Macbeth

Longman Study Texts   General editor: Richard Adams

Titles in the series:

William Shakespeare

Macbeth

edited by
Linda Cookson

with a personal essay by
Braham Murray

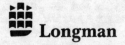 Longman

LONGMAN GROUP UK LIMITED
Longman House
Burnt Mill, Harlow, Essex CM20 2JE, England

First published 1986

ISBN 0 582 33191 9

Set in 10/12 pt Baskerville, Linotron 202

Produced by Longman Group (F.E.) Limited
Printed in Hong Kong

Acknowledgements

Photographs by Donald Cooper

Grose and Oxley, *Shakespeare*, Literature in Perspective Series,
Bell and Hyman, page 256.

Contents

Contents

The director's speech at the first rehearsal – a personal essay

by Braham Murray

Welcome to the first rehearsal of *Macbeth*. This is an exciting day and a terrifying one. Over the next five weeks we're going to grapple with one of the greatest plays ever written. That's exciting, because every day we'll be in close contact with genius. We will be stimulated by an extraordinary energy centre and we will find out through that experience a great deal more about ourselves. It's terrifying, because creatively we shall have to find a way of giving that genius expression.

It is very difficult on the first day of rehearsals to know how much to say about the play. More and more I'm tempted to say nothing and let the voyage take place as we encounter the text in rehearsal. On the other hand, the canvas is so vast, the history of other productions so vivid and the spectrum of interpretation so complex that it seems necessary to say something about why and how we are going to do *Macbeth*. At the worst it will provide a starting point for you to discard as you form your own views.

Why do *Macbeth*? It was written nearly four hundred years ago. It uses a form of language which it is difficult to understand. It's written in verse. It's about the ancient kings of Scotland. It includes, amongst its characters, witches, ghosts and apparitions. All great theatre should illuminate the present and we are not interested in museum productions: we are interested in the problems of today. So why do a play which is so fraught with problems?

I'll try to answer that. But I'll begin by asking another question. Why is *Macbeth* considered to be an unlucky play? Everyone in this room knows that *Macbeth* is so unlucky that its title must not be mentioned in the theatre and it must not be quoted from. The superstition is so strong that I'll bet there isn't a person in this room who is immune to it. I myself have directed this play before, and I can tell you tales of falling pieces of scenery, of a stage manager who fell asleep on the first night ensuring that all the lighting cues were wrong for the whole of the first half, and indeed of attempted suicides. Is there a reason for *Macbeth's* unluckiness, or is it just mindless superstition?

The answer to both these questions is that *Macbeth* is the most brilliant and comprehensive play about evil ever written. Evil is portrayed in its private, public, supernatural and cosmic form. It is a vision of Hell, and during the next five weeks we will be using our imagination to bring that vision to life. We shall cast spells, evoke spirits, pray to demons, murder, intrigue, betray, lie, cheat and pillage. If we are brave enough, we will face the evil in ourselves in order to make the evil in our production true. In doing so we will create in rehearsals an atmosphere that is full of distress and tension which will be conducive to accident and error. We will be bringing into play the dark side of ourselves.

Even more, then, *why* should we do this? Let me give you a quotation or two.

> by the clock 't is day,
> And yet dark night strangles the travelling lamp.
> Is 't night's predominance, or the day's shame,
> That darkness does the face of earth entomb,
> When living light should kiss it?
>
> (Act 2, Scene 4, lines 6–10)

It sounds, does it not, like the description of the nuclear winter? Of how many countries in the world is this true for today, let alone for the time of Hitler's Germany or Stalin's Russia?

Alas, poor country!
Almost afraid to know itself. It cannot
Be called our mother, but our grave; where nothing,
But who knows nothing, is once seen to smile;
Where sighs, and groans, and shrieks that rend the air
Are made, not marked; where violent sorrow seems
A modern ecstasy: the dead man's knell
Is there scarce asked for who; and good men's lives
Expire before the flower in their caps,
Dying or ere they sicken.

(Act 4, Scene 3, lines 164–73)

Do you recognize Chile, South Africa or the missing thousands of Argentina? Shakespeare shows us a society in a state of chaos directly comparable to our time. Not only does he make it vivid to us through the graphic quality of his imagery, but he will not spare us the brutal actuality of it. We have to witness the callous murder of Lady Macduff's son in front of our eyes. We must accept with her:

But I remember now
I am in this earthly world, where to do harm
Is often laudable, to do good sometime
Accounted dangerous folly.

(Act 4, Scene 2, lines 74–7)

I hope I am not ramming the point home when I say that Shakespeare could be writing about the world in which we live. Well, so do many contemporary writers. Hare, Bond, Brenton, to name but three of the better ones, write about injustice, violence, war and evil. They also write in modern English! I submit that what Shakespeare does is something much more. He shows how the power of evil manifests itself, how it takes over the individual and then the society in which that person lives, and he does it with such perspicacity that we cannot fail to recognize the seeds of evil in *us*. That is the first step in preventing the evil expressing itself outwardly in our dealings with the world. Shakespeare's thesis is that the source of evil is to be found in every human being, and if that human being is in a position of power and the evil in that human being is not resolved then that human being will project his own evil into the world. The image of the holocaust is the externalization of something that is unresolved in each one of us. If we can, as a company, produce a *Macbeth* that puts our audiences properly on guard against the source of evil, then we shall have done something that is really worth doing.

Lady Macbeth says of her husband:

> Yet do I fear thy nature:
> It is too full o' the milk of human kindness
> To catch the nearest way. Thou wouldst be great;
> Art not without ambition, but without
> The illness should attend it: what thou wouldst highly,
> That wouldst thou holily.
>
> (Act 1, Scene 5, lines 16–21)

In other words, he is just like anyone else in the room. We wouldn't be here if we weren't ambitious; we want to succeed but we don't want to do it unfairly. Well, I hope it's just like anyone in this room! But Macbeth is rather more than just like us. Duncan echoes the feelings of the entire court when he says to Macbeth:

> The sin of my ingratitude even now
> Was heavy on me. Thou art so far before,
> That swiftest wing of recompense is slow
> To overtake thee: would thou hadst less deserved,
> That the proportion both of thanks and payment
> Might have been mine! only I have left to say:
> More is thy due than more than all can pay.
>
> (Act 1, Scene 4, lines 15–21)

Macbeth is an exceptional man, full of the virtues and qualities that we associate with goodness. By the way, this is something that we must be wary of in rehearsal. The actor playing Macbeth is playing a hero, not a villain, otherwise there is no tragedy, no sense of waste. This is central to Shakespeare's purpose. He shows the tragedy of the corruption of goodness. Too many actors play Macbeth as a villain. He becomes a villain, certainly, in that he murders and deceives, but he begins as a hero. Therefore we must search the text for every opportunity to demonstrate his capacity for goodness. Drama – and tragedy – depend on conflict. If we do not show him wrestling with the opposing forces of good and evil within himself then the play will have no power and its point will be lost.

How is this man corrupted? What is the insane root that keeps his reason prisoner? I'm sure it's not the weird sisters. After all, Banquo says:

> Good Sir, why do you start, and seem to fear
> Things that do sound so fair?
>
> (Act 1, Scene 3, lines 51–2)

implying, as Macbeth realizes:

> If Chance will have me King, why, Chance may crown me,
> Without my stir.
>
> (Act 1, Scene 3, lines 143–4)

No, the weird sisters have touched a chord which was already there – perhaps in the unconscious, perhaps nearer the surface. We'll find out in rehearsal. The heroic Macbeth is as puzzled as we are:

> why do I yield to that suggestion
> Whose horrid image doth unfix my hair,
> And make my seated heart knock at my ribs
> Against the use of nature?
>
> (Act 1, Scene 3, lines 134–7)

After all, if the crown is coming to him anyway, he does not have to contemplate evil ways of gaining it. Don't we all have dark and unworthy faults, and don't we know that moment of deep shame when someone unwittingly brings them into the light? It's like this for Macbeth: he can admit his guilty impulses to himself. What, then, in spite of all this, turns him into a murderer? The answer to this will lie at the heart of this production, and I believe that answer is love. At the very core of the play's action is the love of a man for a woman. In *Macbeth*, Shakespeare wrote some of the finest love scenes ever; I believe that they are as great as those in *Romeo and Juliet* or *Antony and Cleopatra*, but of course they are seen from a very different angle. This is a love that is so inward-looking and so based on the inadequacy of the lovers without each other that it becomes dangerously obsessive and finally projects its poison outwards. Let us examine this more closely.

You've only got to look at whom I've cast as Lady Macbeth to see what I think of that character. She's beautiful, feminine and almost fragile, not the evil stepmother figure that usually graces our stages. After all, why would anyone say:

> Come, you spirits
> That tend on mortal thoughts, unsex me here,
> And fill me, from the crown to the toe, top-full
> Of direst cruelty! ...
> Come to my woman's breasts,
> And take my milk for gall, you murdering ministers,
> (Act 1, Scene 5, lines 40–3, 47–8)

unless she was worried about being too feminine? This attractive woman can only live through her husband, so she is ambitious for him. This is still true of the vast majority of women in our time. In spite of the welcome strides that have been made, it is still only a minority of women who achieve a better fate. But Lady Macbeth loves her husband too; she simply fears that he is not male enough. By 'male' I mean those somewhat unpleasant attributes of physical bravery unaligned with sensitivity which we call 'macho'. She will have to be man enough for two. She will have to make Macbeth say:

> Bring forth men-children only!
> For thy undaunted mettle should compose
> Nothing but males.
> (Act 1, Scene 7, lines 72–4)

She questions Macbeth's manhood:

> When you durst do it, then you were a man.
>
> (Act 1, Scene 7, line 49)

because she knows his sense of inferiority:

> Pr'ythee, peace.
> I dare do all that may become a man;
> Who dares do more is none.
>
> (Act 1, Scene 7, lines 45–7)

and she persuades him to do the deed even after the great 'If it were done' soliloquy where it is clear that Macbeth, like Claudius in *Hamlet*, knows exactly the difference between good and evil. She succeeds because he loves her and she loves him, and the intensity of her love makes him feel whole and overcomes his sense of morality. I'm sure we've all felt that 'insane root', so we must find in these scenes between them their sexual attraction for each other and their need for each other, even when the deed is done and their happiness forever destroyed –

> Nought's had, all's spent,
> Where our desire is got without content.
>
> (Act 3, Scene 2, lines 4–5)

– the love remains,

> Come on;
> Gentle my lord . . .

> So shall I, love.

> O! full of scorpions is my mind, dear wife!

> Be innocent of the knowledge, dearest chuck,
>
> (Act 3, Scene 2, lines 26–7, 29, 36, 45)

albeit now frightened and lonely.

But Shakespeare goes deeper than this. He wants to show us what happens to human beings who deliberately act in contradiction to what they know to be good. Lady Macbeth is a person of little imagination. She has no idea of how her psyche will rebel at the horror of the deed, and so when it is done, she goes mad. But in Macbeth's case Shakespeare is at pains to show us a highly moral and intelligent being consciously treading 'the primrose way' to damnation. I have already mentioned the 'If it were done' soliloquy, where Macbeth presents the reasons why it is unthinkable to murder Duncan, just as you and I have argued with ourselves when tempted to do the wrong thing. In the very next scene, inspired by Lady Macbeth, he prepares to do the deed although it is clear in the next famous soliloquy ('Is this a dagger') that he is still aware of its horror:

> Now o'er the one half world
> Nature seems dead, and wicked dreams abuse
> The curtained sleep.

> (Act 2, Scene 1, lines 49–51)

But note now how the end has its own inbuilt attraction like a drug. That awful dagger of the mind has on its 'blade and dudgeon gouts of blood,/Which was not so before', as it draws him to Duncan; but still he goes. Then, after he returns, shattered from the murder, comes the great moment which is the turning point in his development, when he realizes the only way in which he can mentally survive what he has done:

> To know my deed, 't were best not know myself.

> (Act 2, Scene 2, line 72)

He takes the decision to estrange himself from his better self in order to deny any part of himself that aspires upwards. Shakespeare is showing us the moment that every tyrant since the world began must have lived through. Every human being is born with a mixture of good and evil, and the drama of life lies in the choice that an individual makes. We tend to think of Hitler and Stalin as totally evil. This is not so. They made a choice like every one of us.

Macbeth makes his choice, and from that moment Shakespeare gives us an inside view of a tyrant's mind so that we know, understand and almost sympathize with the problems that despotism brings to the dispute. If you think this is fanciful, read Solzhenitzyn's *First Circle* and his portrait of the inner workings of Stalin's mind, and compare it with: 'To be thus is nothing,/But to be safely thus', or 'But let the frame of things disjoint, both the worlds suffer,/Ere we will eat our meal in fear', or 'But now I am cabined, cribbed, confined, bound in/To saucy doubts and fears.' How easily this leads to the founding of the KGB, Russia's secret police:

> There's not a one of them, but in his house
> I keep a servant fee'd.
>
> (Act 3, Scene 4, lines 131–2)

or the Gestapo, Hitler's death squad:

> The castle of Macduff I will surprise,
> Seize upon Fife; give to th' edge o' th' sword
> His wife, his babes, and all unfortunate souls
> That trace him in his line.
>
> (Act 4, Scene 1, lines 150–4)

Yet all through this we are never allowed to lose our connection with Macbeth the human being, the extraordinarily imaginative and gifted human being who still knows:

> My strange and self-abuse
> Is the initiate fear, that wants hard use.
>
> (Act 3, Scene 4, lines 142–3)

He knows that he has awakened a hell inside him which must soon find its expression outside him:

> It will have blood, they say, blood will have blood:
> Stones have been known to move, and trees to speak;
> Augurs, and understood relations, have
> By magot-pies and choughs, and rooks, brought forth
> The secret'st man of blood.
>
> (Act 3, Scene 4, lines 122–6)

and that

> I am in blood
> Stepped in so far, that, should I wade no more,
> Returning were as tedious as go o'er.

(Act 3, Scene 4, lines 136–8)

Finally, if you want to understand the mad, defiant, destructive courage of Hitler when he began palpably to lose the war after the Battle of Stalingrad, you can do no better than to read the last speeches of the besieged tyrant in his Scottish equivalent of Hitler's bunker.

Before I leave this cursory glance at Macbeth, let me mention Banquo, who seems to me to be a perfect portrait of those so-called 'decent' men who turn a blind eye to the concentration camps of this world rather than risk their own skins. He is perhaps most like us, and the fact that he earns his own murder because he does not stand up against evil should therefore make us pause and think:

> Thou hast it now, King, Cawdor, Glamis, all,
> As the weird women promised; and, I fear,
> Thou playedst most foully for 't; yet it was said,
> It should not stand in thy posterity;
> But that myself should be the root and father
> Of many kings. If there come truth from them
> (As upon thee, Macbeth, their speeches shine),
> Why, by the verities on thee made good,
> May they not be my oracles as well,
> And set me up in hope? But, hush; no more.

(Act 3, Scene 1, lines 1–10)

I hope I have said enough to convince you that our job is to find the essential humanity of these people in order that our audience should identify with them. Then, as they tread the 'primrose path', so our audience will gain a real understanding both of personal evil and of its public consequences.

Let me briefly turn now to the supernatural element. The

ghosts, like the dagger, will be in Macbeth's mind. Take my word for it, it works sensationally, certainly far better than even the most brilliantly effective scenic coup. Let's face it, the audience knows they aren't really ghosts, whatever you do. What the people watching need is to be allowed to use their own imaginations. As to the apparitions that the witches conjure up, I'd ask you to think of voodoo trances, when the women priests become possessed by spirits which transform them vocally. That's what we'll be doing if our actresses are up to it, because it's real and terrifying. But what about the witches? The truth of the matter is that I don't exactly know the answer to that question. I know what they *shouldn't* be. They shouldn't be faintly ludicrous escapees from a Walt Disney film, nor should they be the historically accurate 'gifted women': neither of these alternatives means anything direct to an audience of the 1980s. What should they be? I have suggested that they do not initiate the evil. They touch the chords that are already there. Shakespeare believed in evil as an actual force and – at the risk of being controversial – so do I. How else can you explain that a world full of people who almost to a man profess to desire peace are on the brink of destroying themselves? There is in all of us an urge to self-destruction (psychiatrists call it the 'death wish') that acts against all rationality, and if given in to, affects all the human beings who come in contact with us. I believe the witches represent this force, and I want us to find a style that makes it clear that, like the Ghosts and Apparitions, they work from within the mind. In the scenes with Macbeth, although he speaks to them as if they are in front of him and he can see them, we will see them behind him insinuating their voices into his head. In the scenes where they are alone they must almost be part of the stage – a natural part, the evil part, full of the joy of evil. Somehow we must make the audience recognize them as the siren voice which is also within us and without us.

I have left almost until the last the very difficult question of characters who represent the power of good in the play.

After all, evil is defeated and – unless you adopt the unwarranted and cynical imposition that some directors have perpetrated on the last scene, that there is no hope at all at the end and that the same cycle of violence will repeat itself – the new regime heralds a time of healing. But Shakespeare has given us precious little to go on to make this power of good at all potent. I believe that he wrote this play at a very dark time in his life and came as near as he ever did to pessimism. However, we will have to work very hard to counterbalance this tendency if the play is not to leave our audience in a state of despair.

For instance, in the scene where the murder is discovered, Macduff must make his difficult scene, beginning with 'O horror! horror! horror!', full of genuine outrage. Even Macbeth, with 'Had I but died an hour before this chance', must mean it, and Malcolm and Donalbain must be seen to be showing great wisdom rather than fear in their flight from the court. In a time of evil, retreat and conservation can be the correct things to do. The mysterious Old Man I have cast with a very distinguished actor who has an in-built spiritual force which gives him an aura of the potency of goodness, and he will need it all to mine the lines:

> God's benison go with you; and with those
> That would make good of bad, and friends of foes!
>
> (Act 2, Scene 4, lines 40–1)

Lady Macduff has an easier task. It would take gross incompetence on our part not to rouse the horror of the audience at her and her son's slaughter.

However, the real burden falls on the England scene. This is a very difficult scene to bring alive, and it's where a director desperately needs two very fine leading men but usually ends up with a young actor who is never going to have much of a career to play Malcolm, and a failed older actor to play Macduff. I think I've done rather better than that, and the prospect of trying to bring it off is therefore an exciting one.

The scene before Ross enters falls into three parts. In the first part there is the suspicion of Malcolm and the genuine grief of Macduff; that's not so difficult. In the second part Malcolm has to convince Macduff, and us, that he is the most appalling tyrant; and as he sickens us with that extravagant list of vices, we notice that Macduff holds Macbeth to be even worse. Finally, in the third part he has to convince Macduff, and us, that he is a great actor and a noble prince. Only if he can take us on that extraordinary journey will his closing speech of the play carry with it the authority and promise that are required. The scene is like a whole play in itself. We shall not shirk it.

Also, towards the end of the play, a whole host of small parts appear for the first time, adding to the weight of the good. Some, like the Doctor ('More needs she the divine than the physician') or old Siward accepting the death of his son for the greater good, are rewarding to play. But what of Menteth, Cathness, Angus and Lenox? They have to carry with them the desire for the healing of the sickness, for the return to health of their country – in other words, the force that impels to the good. This will need a lot of hard work and in the end it may get little direct appreciation from the audience because they will sense something rather than recognize it. You will have to create for yourselves three-dimensional characters so that the audience can 'feel' you in anything you say.

And so to the settings and costumes. I want the play to communicate directly to the audience. I do not want them to escape by thinking it's costume drama or by enjoying elaborate sets which remove it into the world of fantasy. I want them to *listen*. So, like the actors of Shakespeare's day, you will have no set. You will evoke time, place, weather and atmosphere through the acting of the text. And when was there a text that evoked those things as potently as this one?

Fair is foul, and foul is fair:
Hover through the fog and filthy air.

(Act 1, Scene 1, lines 10–11)

What lighting could try to emulate the atmosphere of that? As to your costumes, you will enter the stage as actors of today. And in order to play this play of the seventeenth century about an eleventh-century king, you will add pieces of clothes only if necessary: a sword, a crown, a crucifix, a dressing-gown. We are people of now looking back to then in order to find the moment of the present in the past.

I have said enough. I hope I have made vivid *why* we are doing the play, and I hope I have set enough hares running as to *how* we might do the play. Let me emphasize that these are only some solutions and partial ones at that. I assume that each and every one of you will respond to the text in your unique way so that the finished result may be as rich and varied as possible. There can be nothing as exciting as this adventure. And as we turn to Act 1, Scene 1, line 1, the adventure starts now!

Macbeth

CHARACTERS
in the play

DUNCAN, *King of Scotland*

MALCOLM } *the King's sons*
DONALBAIN }

MACBETH } *Generals of the King's Army*
BANQUO }

MACDUFF }
LENOX }
ROSSE }
MENTETH } *Noblemen of Scotland*
ANGUS }
CATHNESS }

FLEANCE, *Banquo's son*
SIWARD, *Earl of Northumberland, General of the English Forces*
YOUNG SIWARD, *Siward's son*
SEYTON, *an officer, attending Macbeth*
BOY, *Macduff's son*
AN ENGLISH DOCTOR
A SCOTTISH DOCTOR
A SOLDIER
A PORTER
AN OLD MAN

LADY MACBETH
LADY MACDUFF
GENTLEWOMAN, *attending Lady Macbeth*
HECATE
THREE WITCHES

LORDS, GENTLEMEN, OFFICERS, SOLDIERS, MURDERERS,
    ATTENDANTS, AND MESSENGERS
THE GHOST OF BANQUO, AND OTHER APPARITIONS

3 *hurlyburly:* tumult of battle.
5 *ere:* before.
8 *Graymalkin:* a grey cat's name.
9 *Paddock:* a toad's name. The cat and the toad are 'familiars', or demon companions, of the witches.
   Anon!: we are coming at once.
10 *Fair is foul, and foul is fair:* to the witches, what most people would regard as beautiful and good is ugly; instead, they find evil attractive.

Questions

1 In what ways does this opening create suspense? What questions does it make you ask?
2 How does the setting of this scene suggest evil and disorder?
3 Imagine that you were staging this meeting. How would you position the three witches?

Act One

Scene one

An open place.

Thunder and lightning. Enter THREE WITCHES.

1 WITCH
 When shall we three meet again,
 In thunder, lightning or in rain?

2 WITCH
 When the hurlyburly's done,
 When the battle's lost and won.

3 WITCH
 That will be ere the set of sun.   5

1 WITCH
 Where the place?

2 WITCH
     Upon the heath.

3 WITCH
 There to meet with Macbeth.

1 WITCH
 I come, Graymalkin!

ALL
 Paddock calls. – Anon! –
 Fair is foul, and foul is fair: 10
 Hover through the fog and filthy air.

             Exeunt

(I.II)   *Alarm:* military trumpet call.

1–3   *He can . . . the newest state:* judging from his wounded condition, he will be able to give us the latest news of the battle.

4   *hardy:* brave.

5   *'Gainst my captivity:* to prevent my being taken prisoner.

6   *knowledge of the broil:* what you know of the battle.

8   *spent:* exhausted.

9   *choke their art:* make it impossible for each other to swim.

10–12   *Worthy . . . upon him:* a natural traitor – all the vices of mankind swarm and breed within him (like vermin or insects) to make him a villain.

12   *western isles:* Ireland, and the Hebrides.

13   *Kernes and Gallowglasses:* lightly armed foot-soldiers and heavily armed cavalry – both from Ireland.

14   *Fortune . . . smiling:* the goddess of good luck appeared to favour Macdonwald's evil rebellion.

15   *Showed like a rebel's whore:* Fortune is here described as a fickle woman who ultimately deserted Macdonwald, and was unfaithful to him as a prostitute might be.

17   *Disdaining:* scorning.
      steel: sword.

18   *smoked:* steamed with blood.

19   *Valour:* courage (here personified as a god).
      minion: favourite.
      carved out his passage: cut his way through.

Questions

1 What do you learn about the battle from the captain's speech?
2 What contrasts between Macdonwald and Macbeth are drawn in this description?

Scene two

A camp near Forres.

Alarm within. Enter KING DUNCAN, MALCOLM, DONALBAIN, LENOX, *with* ATTENDANTS, *meeting a bleeding* CAPTAIN.

DUNCAN

(To the Lords) What bloody man is that? He can re-
    port,
  As seemeth by his plight, of the revolt
  The newest state.

MALCOLM

              This is the sergeant
  Who, like a good and hardy soldier, fought
  'Gainst my captivity. – *(To the soldier)* Hail, brave
    friend!   5
  Say to the King the knowledge of the broil,
  As thou didst leave it.

CAPTAIN

              Doubtful it stood,
  As two spent swimmers, that do cling together
  And choke their art. The merciless Macdonwald
  (Worthy to be a rebel, for to that   10
  The multiplying villainies of nature
  Do swarm upon him) from the western isles
  Of Kernes and Gallowglasses is supplied;
  And Fortune, on his damnèd quarrel smiling,
  Showed like a rebel's whore: but all's too weak; 15
  For brave Macbeth (well he deserves that name),
  Disdaining Fortune, with his brandished steel,
  Which smoked with bloody execution,
  Like Valour's minion, carved out his passage,
  Till he faced the slave;   20

21 *Which:* who (probably referring to Macbeth).
22 *unseamed ... chaps:* ripped him open from the navel to the jaws.
24 *cousin:* Duncan and Macbeth were grandsons of King Malcolm, whom Duncan had succeeded as King of Scotland.
25-8 *As whence ... Discomfort swells:* the friendly sun rises in the east – but it is also from the east that storms break (and the Norwegians have attacked). In other words, trouble can always arise – even from a situation that seems secure.
28 *Mark:* take note.
29 *justice ... with valour armed:* our army had right on its side, assisted by courage.
30 *skipping:* nimble, quick to run away.
31 *Norweyan lord:* Sweno, King of Norway.
   surveying vantage: seeing his opportunity.
32 *furbished:* fresh.
34 *Yes:* this word is spoken ironically. As the next line reveals, Macbeth and Banquo were no more afraid than eagles would be of sparrows, or a lion would be of a hare.
37 *cracks:* charges of gunpowder.
40 *Except:* unless.
41 *memorise another Golgotha:* make the battlefield as memorable a place of death as Golgotha, where Jesus was crucified.

Questions

1 Count the number of references to blood in this scene so far. What atmosphere do they create?
2 Look carefully at the Captain's three speeches describing Macbeth's actions. The language is deliberately formal, in order to create a special mood that emphasizes Macbeth's nobility and heroism.
   (a) What comparison does the Captain make? What does it add to his account?
   (b) What examples of personification can you find in these speeches? What is their effect?
3 How do the language and layout of the Captain's last speech show you that he is near collapse?

Which ne'er shook hands, nor bade farewell to him,
Till he unseamed him from the nave to the chaps,
And fixed his head upon our battlements.

DUNCAN

O valiant cousin! worthy gentleman!

CAPTAIN

As whence the sun 'gins his reflection,   25
Shipwracking storms and direful thunders break,
So from that spring, whence comfort seemed to
    come,
Discomfort swells. Mark, King of Scotland, mark:
No sooner justice had, with valour armed,
Compelled these skipping Kernes to trust their
    heels,   30
But the Norweyan lord, surveying vantage,
With furbished arms, and new supplies of men,
Began a fresh assault.

DUNCAN

                    Dismayed not this
Our captains, Macbeth and Banquo?

CAPTAIN

                                        Yes;
As sparrows eagles, or the hare the lion.   35
If I say sooth, I must report they were
As cannons overcharged with double cracks;
So they
Doubly redoubled strokes upon the foe:
Except they meant to bathe in reeking wounds,   40
Or memorise another Golgotha,
I cannot tell –
But I am faint; my gashes cry for help.

44–5   *So well ... both:* your noble and generous words are, like the injuries
you have suffered, a sign that you are a good and honourable soldier.
45   *smack:* taste.
46   *Thane:* a Scottish title, next in rank after an Earl.
48   *he ... that:* someone ... who.
seems to: looks as though he is about to.
51   *flout:* insult.
52   *fan our people cold:* turn our people cold with fear.
53   *Norway himself:* the King of Norway.
55   *dismal:* threatening.
56   *Till that:* until.
Bellona's bridgegroom: Macbeth is being compared with Mars, the
Roman god of war and husband of Bellona.
lapped in proof: cased in tough armour.
57   *Confronted ... self- comparisons:* faced Sweno with a courage and skill
equal to his own.
58   *Point:* sword-tip.
59   *Curbing:* checking.
lavish: insolent.

Question

In what ways is Rosse's description of Macbeth similar to the
Captain's?

DUNCAN

So well thy words become thee, as thy wounds:
They smack of honour both. – Go, get him surgeons.   45

Exit CAPTAIN, *attended*

Enter ROSSE *and* ANGUS.

(*Turning*) Who comes here?

MALCOLM

The worthy Thane of Rosse.

LENOX

What a haste looks through his eyes!
So should he look that seems to speak things strange.

ROSSE

God save the King!

DUNCAN

Whence camest thou, worthy thane?

ROSSE

From Fife, great King,   50
Where the Norweyan banners flout the sky
And fan our people cold.
Norway himself, with terrible numbers,
Assisted by that most disloyal traitor,
The Thane of Cawdor, began a dismal conflict;   55
Till that Bellona's bridegroom, lapped in proof,
Confronted him with self-comparisons,
Point against point, rebellious arm 'gainst arm,
Curbing his lavish spirit: and, to conclude,
The victory fell on us; –

DUNCAN

Great happiness!   60

11

62 *craves composition:* seeks peace terms.
63 *deign:* permit.
64 *disbursèd:* paid.
   Saint Colmé's Inch: Inchcolm, an island in the Firth of Forth.
66 *that Thane:* the word 'that' shows that Duncan is about to create a new
   Thane of Cawdor.
67 *bosom interest:* affectionate trust.
   present: immediate.

Questions

1 What impression of Duncan does this scene give you?
2 Duncan's last words ('What he had lost, noble Macbeth hath won')
  echo the Witch's earlier words (Act 1, Scene 1, line 4). What is the
  effect of this dramatically?

ROSSE

That now
Sweno, the Norways' king, craves composition;
Nor would we deign him burial of his men
Till he disbursèd at Saint Colmé's Inch
Ten thousand dollars to our general use.   65

DUNCAN

No more that Thane of Cawdor shall deceive
Our bosom interest. – Go, pronounce his present
    death,
And with his former title greet Macbeth.

ROSSE

I'll see it done.

DUNCAN

What he hath lost, noble Macbeth hath won.   70

Exeunt

Scene three

A heath.

Thunder. Enter THREE WITCHES.

1 WITCH

Where hast thou been, sister?

2 WITCH

Killing swine.

3 WITCH

Sister, where thou?

5 *quoth:* said.
6 *Aroint thee:* go away!
   rump-fed: either fat-bottomed or fed on the best meat.
   ronyon: hag.
7 *master:* captain.
   Tiger: the name of a ship.
9 *like a rat without a tail:* the witch will slip aboard the ship to cast her spell in the form of a rat. Traditionally, however, when witches transformed themselves to animals the likeness was not identical: they lacked tails.
10 *I'll do:* I'll take revenge.
14–17 *I myself . . . card:* I control all the other winds and the harbours they blow upon, from every point of the compass-card.
18 *I'll drain him:* the witches will cast spells on the winds to block off the harbours so that the sailor's ship will not be able to enter a port. This will mean that he is unable to seek fresh water to drink.
19 *Sleep:* Macbeth is also destined to be deprived of sleep.
20 *penthouse lid:* eyelid (which slopes like a roof).
21 *forbid:* cursed, cast out.
22 *sev'n-nights nine time nine:* eighty-one weeks.
23 *peak:* waste away.
24 *bark:* ship.

Questions

1 Explain why the witches have decided to persecute the captain of the 'Tiger'.
2 What examples of the witches' magic can you find on this page?
3 What important limitation on their spells is mentioned at line 24? What does this suggest to you about their power?

1 WITCH

    A sailor's wife had chestnuts in her lap,

    And munched, and munched, and munched: "Give

       me," quoth I: 5

    "Aroint thee, witch!" the rump-fed ronyon cries.

    Her husband's to Aleppo gone, master o' the Tiger:

    But in a sieve I'll thither sail,

    And, like a rat without a tail,

    I'll do, I'll do, and I'll do.   10

2 WITCH

    I'll give thee a wind.

1 WITCH

    Th' art kind.

3 WITCH

    And I another.

1 WITCH

    I myself have all the other;

    And the very ports they blow,   15

    All the quarters that they know

    I' the shipman's card;

    I'll drain him dry as hay:

    Sleep shall neither night nor day

    Hang upon his penthouse lid;   20

    He shall live a man forbid.

    Weary sev'n-nights nine times nine,

    Shall he dwindle, peak and pine:

    Though his bark cannot be lost,

    Yet it shall be tempest-tost.   25

    Look what I have.

2 WITCH

    Show me, show me.

32 *weird:* strange. However, the old English word 'wyrd' meant fate or destiny, which also suggests the Witches' power over people's lives.

33 *Posters:* speedy travellers.

35 *thrice to thine, and thrice to mine:* three steps your way, three steps my way. The witches are dancing in a circle.

37 *the charm's wound up:* the spell is cast.

39 *is 't called:* is it said to be.

40 *attire:* clothing.

42–3 *aught . . . question:* anything of which human beings may ask questions. Traditionally, it was thought dangerous to question evil spirits.

44 *choppy:* chapped.

Questions

1 Three and nine were considered to be magic numbers. What details so far in this scene suggest that they are special numbers for the witches?

2 Lines 28–31 all rhyme with each other. Why do you think this is so?

3 How do Macbeth's first words here echo the very first scene of the play? What is the effect of this?

4 What do the witches look like?

5 Why do you think the witches gesture for Banquo to be silent?

1 WITCH

    Here I have a pilot's thumb,
    Wrecked, as homeward he did come.

Drum within

3 WITCH

    A drum! a drum!   30
    Macbeth doth come.

ALL

    The weird sisters, hand in hand,
    Posters of the sea and land,
    Thus do go about, about:
    Thrice to thine, and thrice to mine,   35
    And thrice again, to make up nine.
    Peace! – the charm's wound up.

Enter MACBETH *and* BANQUO.

MACBETH

    So foul and fair a day I have not seen.

BANQUO

    How far is 't called to Forres? – (*He notices the*
      WITCHES) What are these,
    So withered and so wild in their attire   40
    That look not like th' inhabitants o' the earth
    And yet are on 't? – (*He speaks to the* WITCHES) Live
      you? or are you aught
    That man may question? You seem to understand
      me,
    By each at once her choppy finger laying
    Upon her skinny lips: you should be women,   45
    And yet your beards forbid me to interpret
    That you are so.

50 *hereafter:* in the future.
51 *start:* jump, move abruptly.
53–5 *Are ye . . . show?:* are you unreal illusions, or are you really what you appear to be on the outside?
55–6 *greet . . . royal hope:* you greet Macbeth with his current title ('present grace'), and with the promise of a future title ('noble having') and the possibility of kingship ('royal hope').
57 *That:* so that.
    rapt withal: entranced, absorbed by what you have said.
58 *seeds of time:* seeds from which future events will grow.
60–1 *who neither . . . your hate:* I am not asking for favours from you, nor am I afraid of your scorn.

Questions

1 Describe Macbeth's reaction to the witches' prophecies. What do you imagine he is thinking?
2 What does Banquo's speech to the witches suggest to you about his character?

MACBETH

          Speak, if you can: – what are you?

1 WITCH

  All hail, Macbeth! hail to thee, Thane of Glamis!

2 WITCH

  All hail, Macbeth! hail to thee, Thane of Cawdor!

3 WITCH

  All hail, Macbeth! that shalt be king hereafter.   50

BANQUO

  (*Turning to* MACBETH) Good Sir, why do you start,
    and seem to fear
  Things that do sound so fair? – (*To the* WITCHES) I'
    the name of truth,
  Are ye fantastical, or that indeed
  Which outwardly ye show? My noble partner
  You greet with present grace, and great prediction 55
  Of noble having and of royal hope,
  That he seems rapt withal: to me you speak not.
  If you can look into the seeds of time,
  And say which grain will grow, and which will not,
  Speak then to me, who neither beg nor fear   60
  Your favours nor your hate.

1 WITCH

  Hail!

2 WITCH

  Hail!

3 WITCH

  Hail!

1 WITCH

  Lesser than Macbeth, and greater.   65

67   *get:* be the father of.
70   *imperfect:* leaving much unsaid.
71   *Sinel:* Macbeth's father, the previous Thane of Glamis.
74   *within the prospect of belief:* within the bounds of possibility.
76   *owe:* possess.
      intelligence: information.
77   *blasted heath:* wasteland flattened by lightning and storms.
78   *charge:* order.
81   *corporal:* bodily, made of human flesh.
82   *Would:* if only!
84–5   *the insane root ... prisoner:* a plant that can cause insanity (probably a reference to henbane or hemlock).

Questions

1 What detail in Macbeth's first speech on this page shows that he has not heard of the Thane of Cawdor's treachery?
2 Suppose you were directing a performance of this extract:
   (a) Which of these lines do you think the actors should speak loudly, and which softly?
   (b) Which lines should be spoken quickly?
   (c) Which lines should be spoken slowly?
Explain your decisions.

2 WITCH

Not so happy, yet much happier.

3 WITCH

Thou shalt get kings, though thou be none:
So all hail, Macbeth and Banquo!

1 WITCH

Banquo and Macbeth, all hail!

MACBETH

Stay, you imperfect speakers, tell me more.   70
By Sinel's death, I know I am Thane of Glamis;
But how of Cawdor? the Thane of Cawdor lives,
A prosperous gentleman; and to be king
Stands not within the prospect of belief
No more than to be Cawdor. Say, from whence   75
You owe this strange intelligence? or why
Upon this blasted heath you stop our way
With such prophetic greeting? Speak, I charge you.

WITCHES *vanish*

BANQUO

The earth hath bubbles, as the water has,
And these are of them. – Whither are they
  vanished?   80

MACBETH

Into the air; and what seemed corporal, melted
As breath into the wind. – Would they had stayed!

BANQUO

Were such things here, as we do speak about,
Or have we eaten on the insane root
That takes the reason prisoner?   85

21

91   *personal venture:* courageous risk of your own life. This is a reference to Macbeth's combat with Macdonwald.

92–3 *His wonders ... or his:* Duncan did not know whether to express his own amazement or to speak Macbeth's praises.
     Silenced: indecision over what to say left him dumbstruck.

94   *viewing o'er:* reviewing the events of.

96–7 *Nothing afeard ... images of death:* unafraid of the corpses around you, as you turned living people into grotesque, unnatural statues. This contrasts markedly with Macbeth's terror of the 'horrid image' at line 135 in this scene, and with his later fears of Duncan's dead body and Banquo's ghost.

98   *post:* messenger.

99   *in his kingdom's great defence:* for having defended his kingdom so magnificently.

102 *herald:* usher.

104 *earnest:* pledge, token.

Question

Rosse says that Duncan has proclaimed Macbeth Thane of Cawdor as 'earnest of a greater honour' (line 104). What 'greater honour' might Macbeth now be expecting?

MACBETH

Your children shall be kings.

BANQUO

                                        You shall be king.

MACBETH

And Thane of Cawdor too; went it not so?

BANQUO

To the selfsame tune and words. Who's here?

Enter ROSSE *and* ANGUS.

ROSSE

The king hath happily received, Macbeth,
The news of thy success; and, when he reads   90
Thy personal venture in the rebels' fight,
His wonders and his praises do contend,
Which should be thine, or his. Silenced with that,
In viewing o'er the rest o' the selfsame day,
He finds thee in the stout Norweyan ranks,   95
Nothing afeard of what thyself didst make,
Strange images of death. As thick as hail
Ran post with post; and every one did bear
Thy praises in his kingdom's great defence,
And poured them down before him.

ANGUS

                                        We are sent   100
To give thee, from our royal master, thanks;
Only to herald thee into his sight,
Not pay thee.

ROSSE

And, for an earnest of a greater honour,
He bade me, from him, call thee Thane of
    Cawdor: 105

23

106 *addition:* title.
109 *Who was:* the man who used to be.
110 *heavy judgement:* sentence of death.
111 *combined:* in league.
112 *line:* strengthen (a metaphor from sewing).
    the rebel: Macdonwald.
113 *vantage:* support.
114 *laboured in his country's wrack:* plotted to ruin his country.
115 *capital:* carrying the death penalty.
120 *trusted home:* believed absolutely.
121 *enkindle you:* fire, excite your hopes.
123 *to win us to our harm:* to incite us to our own destruction.

Questions

1 What does Banquo mean by 'What! can the devil speak true?' (line 107)?

2 Macbeth says to Banquo: 'Do you not hope your children shall be kings?' (line 118). This is already the second time he has mentioned this prophecy. Why do you think it is particularly on his mind?

3 One of the themes of *Macbeth* is the difference between appearance and reality, between how people *look* and what they really *are*. One set of images that is often used to express this theme is connected with clothes. What two examples of this kind of imagery can you find on this page?

In which addition, Hail! most worthy thane,
For it is thine.

BANQUO

What! can the devil speak true?

MACBETH

The Thane of Cawdor lives: why do you dress me
In borrowed robes?

ANGUS

Who was the thane lives yet;
But under heavy judgement bears that life   110
Which he deserves to lose. Whether he was
combined
With those of Norway, or did line the rebel
With hidden help and vantage, or that with both
He laboured in his country's wrack, I know not;
But treasons capital, confessed and proved,   115
Have overthrown him.

MACBETH

(*Aside*) Glamis, and Thane of Cawdor:
The greatest is behind. (*To* ROSSE *and* ANGUS) Thanks
for your pains.
(*To* BANQUO) Do you not hope your children shall be
kings,
When those that gave the Thane of Cawdor to me
Promised no less to them?

BANQUO

That, trusted home,   120
Might yet enkindle you unto the crown
Besides the Thane of Cawdor. But 't is strange:
And oftentimes, to win us to our harm,
The instruments of darkness tell us truths,

25

125-6 *Win us . . . consequence:* gain our confidence with correct information about trivial things in order to deceive us over things that *really* matter.

126 *Cousins:* friends. The word 'cousins' did not have to apply to blood relations but could be used generally.

128 *prologues:* introductions (a theatrical image).
swelling: increasing in splendour.

129 *imperial:* royal.

130 *soliciting:* prompting.

131 *ill:* evil.

132 *earnest of success:* proof that it will be accurate.

133 *Commencing in:* by beginning with.

134 *suggestion:* temptation.

135 *unfix my hair:* make my hair stand on end.

136 *seated:* firmly fixed within my body.

137 *Against the use of nature:* in an unnatural way.
Present fears: causes for fear which already exist.

138 *less:* less terrifying.

139 *whose murder yet is but fantastical:* in which murder is still only imaginary.

140-1 *Shakes so . . . in surmise:* so disrupts my harmony and balance as an individual (Macbeth is comparing himself to a kingdom or 'state', that should be stable and united) that my ability to act in the present is totally blocked by my constant speculations about the future.

141-2 *nothing is . . . is not:* all that exists for me is imaginary. Only the prospect of kingship (which is fantasy, not fact) is 'real' to Macbeth.

145-6 *Like our strange garments . . . aid of use:* just as new clothes only fit the body comfortably after being worn for some time.

Questions

1 Macbeth seems to imagine himself as the hero in a play about a king. Explain the acting images in lines 127-9.

2 What do you think is the 'suggestion' (line 134) that is now forming in Macbeth's mind?

3 A speech in which a character expresses his or her own thoughts unheard by – or in the absence of – other characters, is known as a *soliloquy*. In *Macbeth* it is often through soliloquies that we become aware of the characters' deepest and most private feelings. What do you learn about Macbeth's character from the soliloquy on this page?

4 What does Banquo suggest as the reason for Macbeth's strange withdrawal?

Win us with honest trifles, to betray 's   125
In deepest consequence. –
(*To* ROSSE *and* ANGUS) Cousins, a word, I pray you.

MACBETH

                  (*Aside*) Two truths are told
As happy prologues to the swelling act
Of the imperial theme. (*To* ROSSE *and* ANGUS) I
   thank you, gentlemen –
(*Aside*) This supernatural soliciting   130
Cannot be ill; cannot be good: – if ill,
Why hath it given me earnest of success,
Commencing in a truth? I am Thane of Cawdor:
If good, why do I yield to that suggestion
Whose horrid image doth unfix my hair,   135
And make my seated heart knock at my ribs
Against the use of nature? Present fears
Are less than horrible imaginings.
My thought, whose murder yet is but fantastical,
Shakes so my single state of man, that function   140
Is smothered in surmise, and nothing is,
But what is not.

BANQUO

        (*To the Lords*) Look, how our partner's rapt.

MACBETH

(*Aside*) If Chance will have me king, why, Chance
   may crown me,
Without my stir.

BANQUO

          New honours come upon him
Like our strange garments, cleave not to their
   mould   145
But with the aid of use.

147   *Time and the hour . . . day:* the stormiest day will always come to an end.
148   *stay upon your leisure:* are waiting for when you are ready to come with us.
149   *Give me your favour:* please excuse me.
      wrought: agitated.
150   *things forgotten:* things I was trying to remember, or things in the past.
      pains: courtesies.
151–2   *registered . . . read them:* recorded in the book of memory and recalled every day.
153   *chanced:* happened by chance.
      at more time: when we have longer.
154   *The interim having weighed it:* having considered it in the meantime.
155   *Our free hearts:* freely, sincerely.

Questions

1 This scene introduces Macbeth to you for the first time. Is he as you expected?
2 Both Macbeth and Banquo have been promised exciting things by the witches. How would you explain the fact that only Macbeth is still brooding about the prophecies, and that only he has been prompted to consider violence?

---

2   *Those in commission:* the messengers given the warrant to command the execution.

MACBETH

> (*Aside*) Come what come may,
> Time and the hour runs through the roughest day.

BANQUO

Worthy Macbeth, we stay upon your leisure.

MACBETH

(*To the Lords*) Give me your favour: my dull brain
   was wrought
With things forgotten. Kind gentlemen, your pains 150
Are registered where every day I turn
The leaf to read them. – Let us toward the king. –
(*To* BANQUO) Think upon what hath chanced; and
   at more time,
The interim having weighed it, let us speak
Our free hearts each to other.

BANQUO

> Very gladly.   155

MACBETH

Till then, enough. – (*To All*) Come, friends.

> *Exeunt*

Scene four

Forres. A room in the King's palace.

Flourish of trumpets. Enter DUNCAN, MALCOLM, DONALBAIN,
LENOX, *and* ATTENDANTS.

DUNCAN

Is execution done on Cawdor? Are not
Those in commission yet returned?

2 *My liege:* my lord.

6 *set forth:* showed.

8 *Became:* befitted. Cawdor died with more dignity and nobility than he lived.

9 *As one . . . in his death:* like someone who had learnt by heart how to
· die – as an actor would rehearse for a death scene.

10 *dearest thing he owed:* his most valuable possession – his life.

11 *careless:* worthless.
   art: skill, technique.

12 *To find . . . in the face:* to discover people's inner thoughts from their outward expressions.

16–18 *Thou art . . . overtake thee:* your merit puts you so far ahead that even the promptest reward is inadequate to match you.

19–20 *That the proportion . . . been mine:* so that I could have thanked and rewarded you in proportion to what you deserve.

21 *thy due:* due to you.
   more than all: more than all I possess.

23 *pays itself:* is its own reward.

25 *children and servants:* like children and servants – affectionate, loyal and respectful.

Question

When an audience watching a play knows more than one of the characters, and is therefore able to see when that character is making mistakes, the playwright is using a technique that is known as *dramatic irony*. Explain the dramatic irony of Duncan's words as Macbeth enters.

MALCOLM
                            My liege,
They are not yet come back; but I have spoke
With one that saw him die: who did report
That very frankly he confessed his treasons,   5
Implored your highness' pardon, and set forth
A deep repentance. Nothing in his life
Became him like the leaving it: he died
As one that had been studied in his death,
To throw away the dearest thing he owed   10
As 't were a careless trifle.

DUNCAN
                      There's no art
To find the mind's construction in the face:
He was a gentleman on whom I built
An absolute trust –

Enter MACBETH, BANQUO, ROSSE, *and* ANGUS.

   (*To* MACBETH) O worthiest cousin!
The sin of my ingratitude even now   15
Was heavy on me. Thou art so far before,
That swiftest wing of recompense is slow
To overtake thee: would thou hadst less deserved,
That the proportion both of thanks and payment
Might have been mine! only I have left to say: 20
More is thy due than more than all can pay.

MACBETH
The service and the loyalty I owe,
In doing it, pays itself. Your highness' part
Is to receive our duties: and our duties
Are, to your throne and state, children and
   servants;
                                                                25

26 *but;* only.
27 *Safe toward:* with a sure regard for.
28 *plant thee:* in making Macbeth Thane of Cawdor, Duncan is preparing him for further advancements in the natural course of things.
31 *infold:* embrace.
33 *The harvest is your own:* you will reap the results.
34 *Wanton:* unrestrained.
35 *drops of sorrow:* tears (which are usually sad).
36 *places:* positions.
    nearest: nearest to the throne.
37 *We:* I. This is an example of the royal plural.
    establish our estate: settle the royal succession.
38 *eldest:* eldest son.
40 *Not, unaccompanied ... only:* he will not be the only person to receive honours.
41 *signs of nobleness:* titles and honours.
41–2 *shall shine ... deservers:* will be distributed widely to all who deserve them.
42 *Inverness:* Macbeth's castle is at Inverness.
43 *bind us further to you:* increase my debt to you (since Macbeth will be Duncan's host).
44 *The rest ... for you:* free time which I do not use in your service gives me no pleasure.
45 *harbinger:* forerunner; the official who preceded a royal visit to make arrangements.
45–6 *make joyful ... your approach:* gladden my wife with the news of your arrival.

Questions

1 In ancient Scotland, the king's eldest son did not automatically succeed to the throne: the king could choose his heir from among any of his close relations. Bearing this in mind, what do you think is the effect on Macbeth of Duncan's announcement at lines 37–9?

2 Shakespeare wishes to present Duncan's rule in Scotland as something natural, harmonious and fruitful. What images on this page are used to create this impression?

Which do but what they should, by doing every-
    thing
Safe toward your love and honour.

DUNCAN

                          Welcome hither:
I have begun to plant thee, and will labour
To make thee full of growing. (*To* BANQUO) – Noble
    Banquo,
That hast no less deserved, nor must be known   30
No less to have done so, let me infold thee,
And hold thee to my heart.

BANQUO

                  There if I grow,
The harvest is your own.

DUNCAN

               My plenteous joys,
Wanton in fulness, seek to hide themselves
In drops of sorrow. – (*To All*) Sons, kinsmen,
    thanes,   35
And you whose places are the nearest, know,
We will establish our estate upon
Our eldest, Malcolm; whom we name hereafter
The Prince of Cumberland: which honour must
Not, unaccompanied, invest him only,   40
But signs of nobleness, like stars, shall shine
On all deservers – (*To* MACBETH) From hence to
    Inverness,
And bind us further to you.

MACBETH

The rest is labour, which is not used for you:
I'll be myself the harbinger, and make joyful   45

48–9   *That is a step . . . fall down:* Malcolm's promotion will trip me up.

49   *o'erleap:* jump over, overcome.

50   *Stars, hide your fires!:* Macbeth's evil thoughts are too wicked for light to shine on them. Murder is a deed of darkness.

52–3   *The eye wink . . . to see:* Let the eye not see what the hand is doing. Yet still allow the deed to be done – even though the eye is afraid to look at the results (i.e., to view the corpse).

54   *True, worthy Banquo:* now that Macbeth has left the stage we can hear the conversation that Duncan and Banquo have been holding in the background throughout the soliloquy.

      full so: so very.

55   *in his commendations I am fed:* hearing him praised is like a feast to me.

57   *care:* thoughtfulness.

58   *It:* he.

      peerless: without equal.

Questions

1 What mood do you think Macbeth is in at lines 48–53? How would you suggest that an actor should approach this speech?

2 'We should not pity Duncan. He is foolish to be so trusting.' Does what you have heard and watched in this scene make you agree or disagree with this comment?

---

1   *They:* the witches.

  success: victory.

2   *by the perfect'st report:* by the most reliable information.

The hearing of my wife with your approach;
So, humbly take my leave.

DUNCAN

My worthy Cawdor!

MACBETH
(*Aside*) The Prince of Cumberland! – That is a step
On which I must fall down, or else o'erleap,
For in my way it lies. Stars, hide your fires!   50
Let not light see my black and deep desires;
The eye wink at the hand, yet let that be,
Which the eye fears, when it is done, to see.

Exit

DUNCAN
True, worthy Banquo, he is full so valiant,
And in his commendations I am fed;   55
It is a banquet to me. Let's after him,
Whose care is gone before to bid us welcome:
It is a peerless kinsman.

Flourish. Exeunt

Scene five

Inverness. A room in MACBETH'S *castle.*

Enter LADY MACBETH, *reading a letter.*

LADY MACBETH
"They met me in the day of success; and I have
learnt by the perfect'st report, they have more in
them than mortal knowledge. When I burned in desire to question them further, they made themselves

35

6 *missives:* messengers.
8 *saluted:* greeted.
8–9 *referred me . . . of time:* revealed the future to me.
10 *deliver thee:* report to you.
12 *dues of rejoicing:* your share of the joy.
17 *milk of human kindness:* the compassion that is part of human nature, and has passed from generation to generation. As Lady Macbeth's later speech shows (lines 47–8), she sees 'milk' as suggesting unwanted and effeminate weakness. She does not consider its life-giving properties.
18 *catch the nearest way:* seize on by the most direct method.
    wouldst be: would like to be.
20 *The illness should attend it:* the evil that ought to accompany it.
    wouldst highly: would very much like. 'Highly' also reminds us that Macbeth is seeking a 'high' position.
21 *That wouldst thou holily:* you would like to gain it without sinning.
    play false: cheat.
22 *wrongly win:* win what you should not have, or win unfairly without having cheated actively.
23 *That which . . . have it:* the thing – the crown – which cries 'You must do this!' if you want it.
24–5 *And that . . . be undone:* you also want the other thing – the murder – to happen: your hesitation is because you fear the deed itself, not because you do not want it done.
25 *Hie thee:* hurry.
26 *pour my spirits in thine ear:* persuade you, communicate my own mood and feelings to you.
27 *chastise:* whip, overcome.
    valour of my tongue: daring of my words.
28 *impedes:* hinders.
    golden round: crown.
29 *metaphysical:* supernatural.
30 *withal:* with.

Questions

1 What do you learn from this speech about Lady Macbeth's opinion of her husband? From what you know of him so far, do you think she is right?
2 What do you think should be the expression on Lady Macbeth's face when the Messenger delivers his news?

air, into which they vanished. Whiles I stood rapt in   5
the wonder of it, came missives from the king, who
all-hailed me 'Thane of Cawdor'; by which title,
before, these weird sisters saluted me, and referred
me to the coming-on of time, with 'Hail, king that
shalt be!' This have I thought good to deliver thee,   10
my dearest partner of greatness, that thou might'st
not lose the dues of rejoicing, by being ignorant of
what greatness is promised thee. Lay it to thy heart,
and farewell."
Glamis thou art, and Cawdor; and shalt be   15
What thou art promised. – Yet do I fear thy nature:
It is too full o' the milk of human kindness
To catch the nearest way. Thou wouldst be great;
Art not without ambition, but without
The illness should attend it: what thou wouldst
　　highly,   20
That wouldst thou holily; wouldst not play false,
And yet wouldst wrongly win; thou 'dst have, great
　　Glamis,
That which cries, "Thus thou must do, if thou have it";
And that which rather thou dost fear to do,
Than wishest should be undone. Hie thee hither,   25
That I may pour my spirits in thine ear,
And chastise with the valour of my tongue
All that impedes thee from the golden round,
Which fate and metaphysical aid doth seem
To have thee crowned withal. –

Enter a MESSENGER.

What is your tidings?   30

MESSENGER
The king comes here tonight.

37

32 *were 't so:* if that were the case.

33 *informed for preparation:* let me know in advance, so that I could prepare.

35 *had the speed of:* outrode.

36 *more:* more breath.

37 *Give him tending:* look after him.

38 *raven:* a bird of ill omen.

41 *unsex me:* remove my femininity.

42 *crown:* head, but the word also reminds us that Lady Macbeth wants to become Queen.
top-full: full up.

44 *Stop up . . . remorse:* block up the route that pity might try to take in order to change my mind. Her blood will be too 'thick' (43) to allow pity to flow through her veins.

45 *compunctious visitings of nature:* natural feelings of conscience.

46 *Shake:* alter.
fell purpose: ruthless plan or intention.

46–7 *keep peace . . . and it:* come between my plan and the action itself.

48 *take my milk for gall:* replace my milk with bitter poison.
ministers: evil spirits.

49 *sightless substances:* invisible forms.

50 *wait on nature's mischief:* assist the evil forces in nature.

51 *pall:* shroud.
dunnest: darkest.

53 *blanket of the dark:* this image combines with 'thick' (50) to give darkness a tangible presence.

54 *Hold:* stop.

Questions

1 Lady Macbeth's phrase 'the all-hail, hereafter' is a haunting reminder of the witches' greeting: 'All hail, Macbeth! that shalt be king hereafter'. In what ways could she herself be described as witch-like?

2 Lady Macbeth says '*my* battlements' (line 40) and '*my* keen knife' (line 52). What do these details suggest?

LADY MACBETH

                         Thou 'rt mad to say it.
Is not thy master with him? who, were 't so,
Would have informed for preparation.

MESSENGER

So please you, it is true: our thane is coming;
One of my fellows had the speed of him,   35
Who, almost dead for breath, had scarcely more
Than would make up his message.

LADY MACBETH

                      Give him tending:
He brings great news. (*Exit* MESSENGER) The raven
   himself is hoarse
That croaks the fatal entrance of Duncan
Under my battlements. Come, you spirits   40
That tend on mortal thoughts, unsex me here,
And fill me, from the crown to the toe, top-full
Of direst cruelty! make thick my blood,
Stop up th' access and passage to remorse;
That no compunctious visitings of nature   45
Shake my fell purpose, nor keep peace between
Th' effect and it! Come to my woman's breasts,
And take my milk for gall, you murdering ministers,
Wherever in your sightless substances
You wait on nature's mischief! Come, thick night, 50
And pall thee in the dunnest smoke of hell,
That my keen knife see not the wound it makes,
Nor heaven peep through the blanket of the dark
To cry, "Hold, hold!"

Enter MACBETH.

               Great Glamis! worthy Cawdor!
Greater than both, by the all-hail, hereafter!   55

56 *transported:* carried.
57 *ignorant:* lacking knowledge of the future.
58 *in the instant:* at this moment.
60 *as he purposes:* so he intends. (In what tone of voice do you think Macbeth makes this remark?)
63 *beguile the time:* deceive the people around you.
64 *Look like the time:* wear an expression that suits the occasion.
   bear welcome: appear welcoming.
67 *provided for:* attended to.
68 *despatch:* management (with a sinister pun on the verb 'to despatch', which means to kill).
70 *solely:* only.
   sovereign sway: kingship.
71 *look up clear:* look at me directly. (Why do you think Macbeth is looking away?)
72 *alter favour:* change the expression in your face.

Questions

1 Lady Macbeth speaks of Duncan as 'He that's coming' (line 66), and says that he will be 'provided for' (line 67) in the night's 'business' (line 68). What does she mean? Why doesn't she speak directly?

2 Why is it appropriate that Lady Macbeth should speak of being a 'serpent' (line 66)?

3 Discuss the relationship between husband and wife in this scene. Do you think they are well matched?

Thy letters have transported me beyond
This ignorant present, and I feel now
The future in the instant.

MACBETH

                    My dearest love,
Duncan comes here tonight.

LADY MACBETH

                    And when goes hence?

MACBETH

Tomorrow, as he purposes.

LADY MACBETH

                O! never   60
Shall sun that morrow see!
Your face, my thane, is as a book, where men
May read strange matters. To beguile the time,
Look like the time, bear welcome in your eye,
Your hand, your tongue: look like the innocent
   flower   65
But be the serpent under 't. He that's coming
Must be provided for; and you shall put
This night's great business into my despatch;
Which shall to all our nights and days to come
Give solely sovereign sway and masterdom.   70

MACBETH

We will speak further.

LADY MACBETH

                Only look up clear;
To alter favour ever is to fear.
Leave all the rest to me.

                        Exeunt

(I.VI) *Hautboys and torches:* music and light contrast with the discord and darkness evoked by the previous scene. Hautboys: oboes.

1 *seat:* situation.

2 *Nimbly:* freshly.

2–3 *recommends itself . . . senses:* soothes and delights us with its touch and fragrance.

4 *temple-haunting martlet:* the house-martin (a bird) traditionally nests in churches.
approve: gives proof.

5 *loved mansionry:* the nests that it likes to build here.

6 *wooingly:* invitingly.
jutty: projection.

7 *coign of vantage:* convenient corner.

7–8 *but this bird Hath:* where this bird has not.

8 *pendent:* hanging.
procreant cradle: nest for breeding.

11–14 *The love . . . your trouble:* the love my subjects have for me can sometimes be a nuisance, but I am still grateful for it because it is love. Although my visit is causing you inconvenience ('pains'), the extra work ('trouble') is being asked of you out of the best of motives. I hope that you will ask God to reward ('yield') me for causing you trouble in such a way – for it proves how much I love you.

15 *point:* respect.

16 *single:* feeble.
contend: compete.

Questions

1 Read carefully Banquo's description of the outside of the castle (lines 4–10). This is to be our last glimpse of normality for some time. What features in the description create a picture of harmony, naturalness and goodness?

2 'Martlet' – or 'martin' – was also Elizabethan slang for a dupe, a person who is too trusting and is deceived. What is the significance of this detail?

Scene six

The same. Before the castle. Hautboys and torches.

Enter DUNCAN, MALCOLM, DONALBAIN, BANQUO, LENOX,
MACDUFF, ROSSE, ANGUS, *and* ATTENDANTS.

DUNCAN

This castle hath a pleasant seat; the air
Nimbly and sweetly recommends itself
Unto our gentle senses.

BANQUO

                  This guest of summer,
The temple-haunting martlet, does approve,
By his loved mansionry, that the heaven's breath   5
Smells wooingly here: no jutty, frieze,
Buttress, nor coign of vantage, but this bird
Hath made his pendent bed, and procreant cradle:
Where they most breed and haunt, I have observed,
The air is delicate.

Enter LADY MACBETH.

DUNCAN

               See, see! our honoured hostess. – 10
(*To* LADY MACBETH) The love that follows us some-
   time is our trouble,
Which still we thank as love. Herein I teach you,
How you shall bid God yield us for your pains,
And thank us for your trouble.

LADY MACBETH

                  All our service,
In every point twice done, and then done double, 15
Were poor and single business to contend
Against those honours deep and broad, wherewith

18 *those of old:* former honours.
19 *late:* recent.
    to: in addition to.
20 *rest your hermits:* remain offering grateful prayers to you. Hermits, or
    beadsmen, offered prayers for the souls of their benefactors.
21 *coursed him at the heels:* followed him closely, as a hare is coursed.
    purpose: plan, intention.
22 *purveyor:* official who goes ahead to arrange provisions for a royal visit.
23 *love:* love for Lady Macbeth.
    holp: helped.
25 *servants:* subjects. Lady Macbeth means herself and Macbeth.
26 *theirs:* their own servants.
    in compt: on account. The King *owns* everything.
27 *make their audit:* account for what the King has entrusted them with.
    at your highness' pleasure: whenever you wish.
28 *Still to return your own:* and can always give back what belongs to you.
30 *graces:* favours.
31 *By your leave:* allow me. He leads her into the castle.

Question

Duncan asks 'Where's the Thane of Cawdor? (line 20). Why do you
think Macbeth is not present during this scene?

(I.VII) *Sewer:* chief server.
         divers: various.
1–2 *If it were . . . done quickly:* if it could all be over and done with for good
     once the deed itself has been committed, then it would be a good thing
     to do it quickly.

44

Your majesty loads our house: for those of old,
And the late dignities heaped up to them,
We rest your hermits.

DUNCAN
                              Where's the Thane of Cawdor? 20
We coursed him at the heels, and had a purpose
To be his purveyor: but he rides well;
And his great love, sharp as his spur, hath holp him
To his home before us. Fair and noble hostess,
We are your guest tonight.

LADY MACBETH
                              Your servants ever   25
Have theirs, themselves, and what is theirs, in
    compt,
To make their audit at your highness' pleasure,
Still to return your own.

DUNCAN
                              Give me your hand;
Conduct me to mine host: we love him highly,
And shall continue our graces towards him.   30
By your leave, hostess.

                                                   Exeunt

Scene seven

The same. A room in the castle. Hautboys and torches.

Enter, and pass over the stage, a SEWER, *and divers* SERVANTS
with dishes and service. Then enter MACBETH.

MACBETH
    (*Aside*) If it were done when 't is done, then 't
    were well

45

2 *assassination:* murder of Duncan.

3 *trammel up the consequence:* prevent further consequences. 'Trammel up' means to entangle or enmesh, as in a net.
catch: secure.

4 *his surcease:* Duncan's death.
that but this blow: if this blow alone.

5 *here:* in this world.

6 *bank and shoal of time:* the human world is seen as a sandbank in the sea of eternity.

7 *jump:* ignore.
life to come: life after death. Macbeth is prepared to risk eternal damnation.
these cases: cases of murder.

8 *have judgement here:* receive sentence on earth.

8–10 *that we but teach ... th' inventor:* in that we only teach others how to kill, and they can then practise that skill on us. In other words, by setting an example of murder by the killing of Duncan, Macbeth will be encouraging someone to avenge Duncan's death by a further murder (of Macbeth himself).

11–12 *commends ... our own lips:* makes us drink from our own cup of poison.

14 *strong both:* both of these factors are strong reasons.

17 *borne his faculties so meek:* exercised his power so humbly.

18 *so clear in his great office:* so fair and blameless a ruler.

19 *plead:* speak on his behalf. This image – like 'cases' (7), 'judgement' (8) and 'instructions' (9) – comes from the language of lawyers.

20 *damnation of his taking-off:* mortal sin of his murder.

22 *Striding the blast:* bestriding the storm of fury (that so evil and unnatural a murder would provoke).
cherubin: an order of angels, often depicted as little children.
horsed: riding.

23 *sightless couriers:* invisible messengers, i.e., the winds.

24–5 *Shall blow ... drown the wind:* the knowledge of this murder will be blown like dust into people's eyes, causing them to weep, so that the tears of all humanity will drown the storm.

25–6 *I have no spur ... of my intent:* I have nothing to spur on my purpose (as a rider spurs on a horse).

27–8 *Vaulting ambition ... on the other:* bounding ambition, which leaps too eagerly into the saddle and falls on the other side.

Questions

1 What reasons does Macbeth give here for not killing Duncan?

2 What do the images that Macbeth uses to express his thoughts in this soliloquy reveal about his state of mind?

3 Duncan 'has almost supped' (line 29). Like Judas, Macbeth has left his victim at supper. What other imagery drawn from Christianity have you noticed in the play so far?

It were done quickly: if the assassination
Could trammel up the consequence, and catch
With his surcease success; that but this blow
Might be the be-all and the end-all here,   5
But here upon this bank and shoal of time,
We'd jump the life to come, – But, in these cases,
We still have judgement here, that we but teach
Bloody instructions, which, being taught, return
To plague th' inventor: this even-handed justice   10
Commends th' ingredients of our poisoned
    chalice
To our own lips. He's here in double trust:
First, as I am his kinsman and his subject,
Strong both against the deed; then, as his host,
Who should against his murderer shut the door,   15
Not bear the knife myself. Besides, this Duncan
Hath borne his faculties so meek, hath been
So clear in his great office, that his virtues
Will plead like angels, trumpet-tongued, against
The deep damnation of his taking-off;   20
And pity, like a naked new-born babe,
Striding the blast, or heaven's cherubin, horsed
Upon the sightless couriers of the air,
Shall blow the horrid deed in every eye,
That tears shall drown the wind. – I have no spur   25
To prick the sides of my intent, but only
Vaulting ambition, which o'erleaps itself
And falls on the other –

Enter LADY MACBETH.

How now! what news?

LADY MACBETH
He has almost supped. Why have you left the
    chamber?

32–3 *bought Golden opinions:* gained the highest respect.
34 *would:* should.
     in their newest gloss: shining like new robes.
35 *Was the hope drunk:* was your optimism only stimulated by drink?
37 *look so green and pale:* appear so sickly and fearful.
38 *At what it did so freely:* at the promises made so readily when drunk.
39 *Such:* like this, i.e., like a drunken promise.
     account: consider.
40–1 *To be the same ... in desire:* to show the same determination in your behaviour and courage as you do in your desires.
41 *that:* the crown.
42 *esteem'st:* judge to be.
43 *esteem:* estimation.
44 *wait upon:* follow.
45 *adage:* proverb. The cat wanted fish from the pond, but did not want to get its paws wet.
46 *become:* befit.
47 *is none:* is not a man at all. He becomes a beast.
48 *break:* propose.
50 *to be more than what you were:* to become King.

Questions

1 What reason does Macbeth give to explain why he no longer wishes to murder Duncan? How does this compare with the reasons he gave in his soliloquy (lines 1–28)?
2 What arguments does Lady Macbeth use to try to change his mind?
3 What different views do Macbeth and his wife have about manliness?
4 Explain the images of clothes that are used in this conversation.

MACBETH
  Hath he asked for me?

LADY MACBETH
                   Know you not he has?   30

MACBETH
  We will proceed no further in this business:
  He hath honoured me of late; and I have bought
  Golden opinions from all sorts of people,
  Which would be worn now in their newest gloss,
  Not cast aside so soon.

LADY MACBETH
                  Was the hope drunk,   35
  Wherein you dressed yourself? hath it slept since,
  And wakes it now, to look so green and pale
  At what it did so freely? From this time
  Such I account thy love. Art thou afeard
  To be the same in thine own act and valour,   40
  As thou art in desire? Wouldst thou have that
  Which thou esteem'st the ornament of life,
  And live a coward in thine own esteem,
  Letting "I dare not" wait upon "I would,"
  Like the poor cat i' the adage?

MACBETH
                      Pr'ythee, peace.   45
  I dare do all that may become a man;
  Who dares do more is none.

LADY MACBETH
                What beast was 't then
  That made you break this enterprise to me?
  When you durst do it, then you were a man;
  And, to be more than what you were, you would   50

51 *more the man:* more courageous.
   Nor . . . nor: neither . . . nor.
52 *Did then adhere:* were suitable at the time you first thought of the undertaking.
   would: were determined to.
53 *They have made themselves:* the opportunity has presented itself.
   that their fitness: their very suitability.
54 *unmake:* destroy your manhood.
59 *We fail?:* Lady Macbeth speaks in scornful disbelief.
60 *But screw . . . sticking-place:* only have courage and achieve exactly the right frame of mind. The 'sticking-place' is the limit to which a soldier tightens the string of his cross-bow before firing. The image could also suggest the tightening of the strings of a violin in order to achieve perfect tuning.
63 *chamberlains:* attendants of the royal bed-chamber.
64 *wassail:* merry-making.
   convince: overcome.
65 *warder:* guard. Memory was thought to be in the lowest part of the brain so that it guarded reason (which was above it) against fumes rising from the stomach.
66-7 *Shall be a fume . . . limbeck only:* memory will dissolve into an alcoholic vapour, so that the brain – the receptacle ('receipt') of reason – will become a retort ('limbeck') used for distilling alcohol.
68 *drenchèd:* soaked in drink.
   as in a death: unconscious.
71 *spongy:* drink-sodden.
72 *quell:* murder.
73 *mettle:* spirit.
74 *received:* believed.
75 *marked:* smeared.

Questions

1 How do you react to Lady Macbeth's speech at lines 54–9? What do you think has prompted her to make this declaration?
2 Lady Macbeth is claiming that the murder will be an act of great courage. What details in the murder plan show that this is not true?

Be so much more the man. Nor time nor place
Did then adhere, and yet you would make both:
They have made themselves, and that their fitness
   now
Does unmake you. I have given suck, and know
How tender 't is to love the babe that milks me: 55
I would, while it was smiling in my face,
Have plucked my nipple from his boneless gums,
And dashed the brains out, had I so sworn as you
Have done to this.

MACBETH

                If we should fail, –

LADY MACBETH

                        We fail?
But screw your courage to the sticking-place   60
And we'll not fail. When Duncan is asleep
(Whereto the rather shall his day's hard journey
Soundly invite him), his two chamberlains
Will I with wine and wassail so convince,
That memory, the warder of the brain,   65
Shall be a fume, and the receipt of reason
A limbeck only: when in swinish sleep
Their drenchèd natures lie, as in a death,
What cannot you and I perform upon
Th' unguarded Duncan? What not put upon   70
His spongy officers, who shall bear the guilt
Of our great quell?

MACBETH

              Bring forth men-children only!
For thy undaunted mettle should compose
Nothing but males. Will it not be received,
When we have marked with blood those sleepy two   75

76 *very:* own.
77 *other:* any other way.
78 *As we ... clamour roar:* since we will make such a great outcry of grief.
79 *settled:* decided.
   bend up: Macbeth is comparing himself to a bow being made ready for shooting.
80 *corporal agent:* bodily power.
   feat: deed.
81 *mock the time:* delude those around us.
   with fairest show: by appearing to be loyal and honest.

Questions

1 Whose fault is it that Macbeth is about to commit a murder?
2 What do you think will happen in Act 2?

Of his own chamber, and used their very daggers,
That they have done 't?

LADY MACBETH

                    Who dares receive it other,
As we shall make our griefs and clamour roar
Upon his death?

MACBETH

                  I am settled, and bend up
Each corporal agent to this terrible feat.   80
Away, and mock the time with fairest show:
False face must hide what the false heart doth know.

Exeunt

1 *How goes the night:* what time of night is it?
3 *Sir:* Fleance addresses his father with respect.
4 *husbandry:* thrift, economy.
5 *Their candles are all out:* the stars have hidden their fires (as Macbeth commanded (Act 1, Scene 4, line 50)). Banquo suggests that heaven is economizing on light.
Take thee that, too: Banquo passes Fleance something else (perhaps a helmet or belt) at this point.
6 *heavy summons:* deep feeling of tiredness.
7 *I would not:* I do not wish to.
merciful powers: angels who ward off evil spirits.
8–9 *Restrain in me . . . in repose:* stop me from experiencing the dreadful nightmares that overwhelm me in my sleep.
9 *Give me my sword:* Banquo becomes agitated when he sees the approaching torchlight.

Questions

1 In what ways does this opening scene arouse tension?
2 Why do you think Banquo has been having bad dreams?

Act Two

Scene one

The same. A court within the castle.

Enter BANQUO, *and* FLEANCE *with a torch before him.*

BANQUO
How goes the night, boy?

FLEANCE
The moon is down; I have not heard the clock.

BANQUO
And she goes down at twelve.

FLEANCE
      I take 't, 't is later, Sir.

BANQUO
Hold, take my sword. – There's husbandry in
 heaven;
Their candles are all out. – Take thee that, too.   5
A heavy summons lies like lead upon me,
And yet I would not sleep: merciful powers!
Restrain in me the cursèd thoughts that nature
Gives way to in repose! – Give me my sword.

Enter MACBETH, *and a* SERVANT *with a torch.*

(*To* MACBETH) Who's there?   10

MACBETH
A friend.

13 *He hath been in unusual pleasure:* he has had an exceptionally enjoyable evening.

14 *largess:* gifts.

offices: servants' quarters.

16 *By the name of:* addressing her as.

shut up: ended the day; went to bed.

17–19 *Being unprepared . . . free have wrought:* we were not warned in advance of the visit, so our desire to entertain Duncan was rather thwarted by this drawback ('defect') – otherwise our hospitality would have been lavish.

19 *All's well:* everything was satisfactory.

22 *entreat an hour to serve:* find a convenient time.

24 *At your kind'st leisure:* whenever you are kind enough to find some time to spare.

25–6 *If you . . . honour for you:* Macbeth is being deliberately vague here. This could mean: if you follow my advice when we have our talk, then that will do you credit. But it could also mean: if you are loyal to my side when it comes into being, it will be to your advantage.

26 *So I lose none:* provided that I lose no honour.

27 *augment:* increase.

still: always.

28 *bosom franchised:* clear conscience.

allegiance clear: unsullied loyalty.

29 *be counselled:* listen to what you have to say.

Questions

1 Traditionally, a diamond was thought to be a lucky charm against witchcraft or possession by demons. Why is it ironic that Duncan should give a diamond to Lady Macbeth?

2 What lie does Macbeth tell in this exchange?

3 Do you see any signs that Banquo is suspicious of Macbeth?

BANQUO

What, Sir! not yet at rest? The king's a-bed:
He hath been in unusual pleasure, and
Sent forth great largess to your offices.
This diamond he greets your wife withal,   15
By the name of most kind hostess, and shut up
In measureless content.

MACBETH

                Being unprepared,
Our will became the servant to defect,
Which else should free have wrought.

BANQUO

                       All's well.

I dreamt last night of the three weird sisters: 20
To you they have showed some truth.

MACBETH

                  I think not of them:
Yet, when we can entreat an hour to serve,
We would spend it in some words upon that busi-
    ness,
If you would grant the time.

BANQUO

                At your kind'st leisure.

MACBETH

If you shall cleave to my consent, when 't is,   25
It shall make honour for you.

BANQUO

             So I lose none
In seeking to augment it, but still keep
My bosom franchised, and allegiance clear,
I shall be counselled.

32   *strike upon the bell*: as line 62 shows, the ringing of the bell is a pre-arranged signal.

35   *I have thee not:* Macbeth has reached out to try to grasp the invisible dagger, which eludes him.

36–7   *sensible . . . sight:* able to be touched as well as seen.

39   *heat-oppressèd:* feverish.

40   *yet:* still.
      palpable: touchable.

41   *this:* Macbeth draws his own dagger from its sheath.

42   *marshall'st:* direct.
      the way that I was going: towards Duncan's room.

43   *to use:* to commit murder with.

44–5   *Mine eyes . . . all the rest:* either my eyes are fools compared with the other senses (for believing what is not real), or else they are superior to all the other senses (by perceiving something that is hidden from the others).

46   *dudgeon:* hilt.
      gouts: drops.

48–9   *informs Thus:* assumes this form.

49   *one half world:* the hemisphere that is in darkness.

50   *abuse:* mock, torment.

51   *curtained:* by eyelids, or by the curtains of a four-poster bed.

52   *Hecate:* goddess of witchcraft.
      withered Murder: murder is personified as a deformed, sterile assassin.

Questions

1 What makes Macbeth see a vision of a dagger?
2 Macbeth knows that the dagger directing him to the murder is an illusion, but he still follows it. What is the significance of this?

MACBETH

Good repose the while!

BANQUO

Thanks, Sir: the like to you.   30

Exeunt BANQUO *and* FLEANCE

MACBETH

(*To the* SERVANT) Go, bid thy mistress, when my
    drink is ready,
She strike upon the bell. Get thee to bed. –

Exit SERVANT

Is this a dagger which I see before me,
The handle toward my hand? (*He speaks to the
    dagger*) Come, let me clutch thee: –
I have thee not, and yet I see thee still.   35
Art thou not, fatal vision, sensible
To feeling as to sight? or art thou but
A dagger of the mind, a false creation,
Proceeding from the heat-oppressèd brain?
I see thee yet, in form as palpable   40
As this which now I draw.
Thou marshall'st me the way that I was going;
And such an instrument I was to use. –
Mine eyes are made the fools o' the other senses,
Or else worth all the rest: I see thee still;   45
And on thy blade and dudgeon gouts of blood,
Which was not so before. – There's no such thing.
It is the bloody business which informs
Thus to mine eyes. – Now o'er the one half world
Nature seems dead, and wicked dreams abuse   50
The curtained sleep: witchcraft celebrates
Pale Hecate's offerings; and withered Murder,

53 *Alarumed:* called up.
    sentinel: sentry.
54 *watch:* watchman's cry.
55 *Tarquin's ravishing strides:* the strides of Tarquin on his way to rape
    Lucretia. Tarquin was a cruel Roman king.
    design: evil purpose.
56 *sure and firm-set:* the solidity of the ground contrasts with the atmosphere
    of nightmare, illusion and ghostliness.
58 *prate of my where-about:* reveal where I am.
59 *take:* remove.
60 *suits with it:* is appropriate to the occasion.
    threat: talk about murder.
62 *the bell invites me:* the signal summons me.
63 *knell:* ringing, usually to mark someone's death.

Questions

1 How does the language of lines 49–60 create an atmosphere of evil
   and nightmare?
2 In what tone of voice do you think an actor should say the last two
   lines of this scene?

---

1 *them:* the chamberlains.
2 *quenched them:* put them out of action (because of drinking too much).
   fire: courage. Lady Macbeth has been drinking to increase her confidence.
   Hark!: Lady Macbeth is startled by the sudden cry of the owl.
3 *owl:* a bird of ill omen, whose shriek was supposed to herald a death.
   fatal bellman: either a reference to bell-ringing at funerals or to the fact that
   a bellman would ring a bell outside the condemned cell just before the
   prisoner's execution.
4 *stern'st good-night:* grimmest farewell.
   about it: doing the deed.
5 *surfeited grooms:* servants who have drunk too much.
6 *mock their charge:* make a mockery of their duty to guard the King.
   possets: hot bedtime drinks, made or milk, wine and spices.

Alarumed by his sentinel, the wolf,
Whose howl's his watch, thus with his stealthy
    pace,
With Tarquin's ravishing strides, towards his
    design   55
Moves like a ghost. – Thou sure and firm-set earth,
Hear not my steps, which way they walk, for fear
Thy very stones prate of my where-about,
And take the present horror from the time,
Which now suits with it. Whiles I threat, he lives: 60
Words to the heat of deeds too cold breath gives.

A bell rings.

I go, and it is done: the bell invites me.
Hear it not, Duncan; for it is a knell
That summons thee to heaven or to hell.

                                            Exit

Scene two

The same.

Enter LADY MACBETH.

LADY MACBETH
That which hath made them drunk hath made me
    bold.
What hath quenched them hath given me fire. –
    Hark! – Peace!
It was the owl that shrieked, the fatal bellman,
Which gives the stern'st good-night. He is about it.
The doors are open, and the surfeited grooms   5
Do mock their charge with snores. I have drugged
    their possets,

7–8   *That death ... live or die:* death and life are quarrelling about who possesses them.
8   *Within:* off-stage.
11   *Confounds:* ruins.
13   *had:* would have.
15   *crickets:* crickets, like owls, were supposed to foretell death.

Questions

1   Why do you think Shakespeare chose not to present Duncan's murder on stage?
2   How is tension created in this scene?
3   What signs are we given here which suggest that Lady Macbeth is not as totally ruthless and inhuman as she would like to be?

That death and nature do contend about them,
Whether they live or die.

MACBETH

        (*Within*) Who's there? – what, ho!

LADY MACBETH

Alack! I am afraid they have awaked,
And 't is not done: – the attempt, and not the deed,   10
Confounds us. – Hark! – I laid their daggers ready;
He could not miss them. – Had he not resembled
My father as he slept, I had done 't. – My husband!

Enter MACBETH.

MACBETH

I have done the deed. – Didst thou not hear a noise?

LADY MACBETH

I heard the owl scream, and the crickets cry.   15
Did not you speak?

MACBETH

        When?

LADY MACBETH

          Now.

MACBETH

           As I descended?

LADY MACBETH

Ay.

MACBETH

    Hark!
Who lies i' the second chamber?

LADY MACBETH

          Donalbain.

20 *sorry:* wretched.
23 *That:* so that.
24 *addressed them:* prepared themselves.
25 *lodged together:* sharing the same chamber. It is possible that this description refers to the two princes, Malcolm and Donalbain. If it does, what is the point of Lady Macbeth's comment here?
27 *As:* as it.
   hangman's hands: hangmen disembowelled victims, as well as hanging them.
28 *Listening:* listening to.
30 *wherefore:* why.
   pronounce: speak the word.
31–2 *'Amen' Stuck in my throat:* inability to pray was a sign of being possessed by devils.
33 *After:* in.
   so: if we do so.
35 *murder sleep:* Duncan was asleep when Macbeth stabbed him.

Questions

1 Explain what has happened to disturb Macbeth so deeply.
2 Why does Macbeth say 'I had most need of blessing' (line 31)?

MACBETH

(*Looking at his hands*) This is a sorry sight. 20

LADY MACBETH

A foolish thought, to say a sorry sight.

MACBETH

There's one did laugh in 's sleep, and one cried,
   "Murder!"
That they did wake each other: I stood and heard
   them;
But they did say their prayers, and addressed them
Again to sleep.

LADY MACBETH

                    There are two lodged together. 25

MACBETH

One cried, "God bless us!" and, "Amen," the other,
As they had seen me with these hangman's hands.
Listening their fear, I could not say, "Amen,"
When they did say, "God bless us!"

LADY MACBETH

                         Consider it not so deeply.

MACBETH

But wherefore could not I pronounce "Amen"? 30
I had most need of blessing, and "Amen"
Stuck in my throat.

LADY MACBETH

                These deeds must not be thought
After these ways: so, it will make us mad.

MACBETH

Methought I heard a voice cry, "Sleep no more!
Macbeth does murder sleep," – the innocent sleep; 35

36 *knits up the ravelled sleave:* smooths out the tangled skein.
37 *bath:* refreshment.
38 *Balm:* soothing ointment.
     course: course of food.
39 *Chief nourisher:* the second course at dinner was the meat course – the most
     filling and substantial.
44 *unbend:* dismantle. See the note to Act 1, Scene 7, line 79, page 52.
45 *brainsickly:* deliriously.
46 *witness:* evidence.
48 *lie:* remain.
51 *Infirm:* unstable.
55 *gild:* make golden.
56 *guilt:* a cynical pun on 'gilt' (a thin layer of gold) with 'guilt' (blame or
     fault).

Questions

1 What has Macbeth forgotten to do?
2 What do you think ought to be the differences in tone between
   Lady Macbeth's three speeches on this page?
3 What does Lady Macbeth mean by lines 52–4 ('The sleeping and
   the dead . . . painted devil')?

Sleep, that knits up the ravelled sleave of care,
The death of each day's life, sore labour's bath,
Balm of hurt minds, great nature's second course,
Chief nourisher in life's feast; –

LADY MACBETH

                What do you mean?

MACBETH

Still it cried, "Sleep no more!" to all the house: 40
"Glamis hath murdered sleep, and therefore Cawdor
Shall sleep no more, Macbeth shall sleep no more!"

LADY MACBETH

Who was it that thus cried? Why, worthy thane,
You do unbend your noble strength, to think
So brainsickly of things. Go, get some water,   45
And wash this filthy witness from your hand. –
Why did you bring these daggers from the place?
They must lie there; go, carry them, and smear
The sleepy grooms with blood.

MACBETH

                   I'll go no more:
I am afraid to think what I have done;   50
Look on 't again I dare not.

LADY MACBETH

                Infirm of purpose!
Give me the daggers. The sleeping and the dead
Are but as pictures; 't is the eye of childhood
That fears a painted devil. If he do bleed,
I'll gild the faces of the grooms withal,   55
For it must seem their guilt.

                                  Exit

56 *Whence:* where from?
57 *How is 't with me:* what's the matter with me?
58 *What hands . . . mine eyes:* an echo of Matthew 18:9 ('And if thine eye cause thee to offend, pluck it out, and cast it from thee').
59 *Neptune:* the Roman god of the sea.
60 *rather:* instead.
61 *multitudinous:* many.
   incarnadine: dye blood-red.
63 *shame:* would be ashamed.
64 *white:* cowardly.
67–8 *Your constancy . . . unattended:* your firmness has deserted you.
69 *night-gown:* dressing gown.
   occasion: circumstances.
70 *watchers:* still awake, up and dressed.
71 *poorly:* weakly, miserably.
72 *To know . . . know myself:* I'd rather not know myself than face up to what I have done.

Questions

1 What differences does this scene reveal between the ways in which Macbeth and Lady Macbeth think?
2 What is the dramatic effect of the knocking at this point?

Knocking within.

MACBETH

                 Whence is that knocking? –
How is 't with me, when every noise appals me?
What hands are here? Ha! they pluck out mine
    eyes.
Will all great Neptune's ocean wash this blood
Clean from my hand? No, this my hand will
    rather   60
The multitudinous seas incarnadine,
Making the green one red.

Re-enter LADY MACBETH.

LADY MACBETH

My hands are of your colour; but I shame
To wear a heart so white. (*Knock*) I hear a knocking
At the south entry: retire we to our chamber.   65
A little water clears us of this deed:
How easy is it then! Your constancy
Hath left you unattended. – (*Knock*) Hark! more
    knocking.
Get on your night-gown, lest occasion call us,
And show us to be watchers. – Be not lost   70
So poorly in your thoughts.

MACBETH

To know my deed, 't were best not know myself.

Knock.

Wake Duncan with thy knocking: I would thou
    couldst!

                                       Exeunt

2 *old:* plenty of (since so many people go to hell).

4 *Beelzebub:* one of the chief devils.

4–5 *hanged himself . . . of plenty:* hoarded grain, expecting the price to rise, and then hanged himself when a good harvest made grain cheap and plentiful.

5–6 *time-server:* someone who serves his own interests. There is also a pun on serving time, in the sense of undergoing imprisonment.

6 *have napkins enough about you:* bring plenty of handkerchiefs (he will sweat in Hell).

8 *the other devil:* he probably means Satan.

equivocator: someone who lies indirectly, by deliberately using ambiguous words. The next few lines carry a topical reference to the trial and hanging of a Father Garnet for his part in the Gunpowder Plot (see 'Studying *Macbeth*', page 238). He had defended himself by equivocation and insisted it was not perjury to do so.

9–10 *that could swear . . . either scale:* his declarations on oath were so ambiguous that it was impossible to establish his true position. The 'scales' are the scales of justice.

14 *stealing out of a French hose:* trying to skimp on material, and stealing whatever fabric he saved. French breeches ('hose') were very tight, however, so the theft was apparent.

15 *roast your goose:* heat your smoothing-iron.

19 *primrose way:* attractive path.

19–20 *everlasting bonfire:* Hell.

20 *Anon, anon:* just a moment – I'm on my way!

21 *remember:* give a tip to.

23 *lie so late:* sleep in.

Questions

1 What job is the Porter pretending to do in his monologue?

2 This speech is an example of *black comedy*, because the humour – although amusing – has a groteque and sinister purpose.

  (a) What does Macbeth's castle have in common with 'hell-gate' (line 2)?

  (b) What do Macbeth and Lady Macbeth have in common with the sinners whom the Porter imagines?

Scene three

The same.

Enter a PORTER.

Knocking within.

PORTER

Here's a knocking indeed! If a man were porter of
hell-gate, he should have old turning the key. (*Knock-ing*) Knock, knock, knock. Who's there, i' the name
of Beelzebub? – Here's a farmer that hanged him-
self on the expectation of plenty; come in time-server;   5
have napkins enough about you; here you'll sweat
for 't. (*Knocking*) Knock, knock. Who's there, i' the
other devil's name? – 'Faith, here's an equivocator
that could swear in both the scales against either
scale; who committed treason enough for God's   10
sake, yet could not equivocate to heaven: O! come
in, equivocator. (*Knocking*) Knock, knock, knock.
Who's there? – 'Faith, here's an English tailor come
hither for stealing out of a French hose: come in,
tailor; here you may roast your goose. (*Knocking*)   15
Knock, knock. Never at quiet! What are you? – But
this place is too cold for hell. I'll devil-porter it
no further: I had thought to have let in some of all
professions that go the primrose way to the everlasting bonfire. (*Knocking*) Anon, anon: I pray you,   20
remember the porter.

Opens the gate.

Enter MACDUFF *and* LENOX.

MACDUFF

Was it so late, friend, ere you went to bed,
That you do lie so late?

24 *the second cock:* about 3 a.m.
27 *nose-painting:* drinking alcohol tends to lead to red noses.
   Lechery: lust.
28 *provokes and unprovokes:* stimulates and spoils.
29 *takes away:* reduces.
30 *equivocator:* trickster, double-dealer.
31 *mars:* destroys.
31-2 *sets him on, and it takes him off:* encourages him and disheartens him.
33-4 *stand to, and not stand to:* (an obscene pun) be ready for action, but
   unable to get an erection.
34 *equivocates him in a sleep:* tricks him into sleeping, or deceives him with
   a dream.
35 *giving him the lie:* showing that he could not do what he said, and/or
   laying him out (like a wrestler).
37 *the very throat o' me:* my very throat. A 'lie in the throat' was a direct
   lie. The Porter is also punning, of course, on the fact that alcohol is
   taken in through the throat.
38 *requited:* repaid.
39 *took up my legs:* a wrestling term to describe alcohol's fight to make him
   too drunk to walk properly.
   sometime: sometimes.
40 *made a shift:* managed.
   cast: throw, like a wrestler – with a pun on 'throw up', or vomit.

Questions

1 What, according to the Porter, are the inconveniences caused by
  drinking too much?
2 What is the effect of the delay before the murder is discovered?

PORTER
'Faith, Sir, we were carousing till the second cock;
And drink, Sir, is a great provoker of three things.   25

MACDUFF
What three things does drink especially provoke?

PORTER
Marry, Sir, nose-painting, sleep and urine. Lechery,
Sir, it provokes and unprovokes: it provokes the
desire, but it takes away the performance. Therefore, much drink may be said to be an equivocator   30
with lechery: it makes him and it mars him; it sets
him on, and it takes him off; it persuades him, and
disheartens him; makes him stand to, and not
stand to: in conclusion, equivocates him in a sleep,
and, giving him the lie, leaves him.   35

MACDUFF
I believe drink gave thee the lie last night.

PORTER
That it did, Sir, i' the very throat o' me: but I
requited him for his lie; and, I think, being too
strong for him, though he took up my legs sometime,
yet I made a shift to cast him.   40

MACDUFF
Is thy master stirring?

Enter MACBETH.

Our knocking has awaked him; here he comes.

LENOX
(*To* MACBETH) Good morrow, noble Sir!

MACBETH
                        Good morrow, both!

45 *timely:* early.
46 *slipped the hour:* missed the time.
47 *this:* the role of host.
48 *one:* a trouble.
49 *The labour ... physics pain:* doing a task we enjoy is a remedy for the trouble involved: our 'pain' is cured.
50 *limited service:* appointed task.
51 *appoint:* arrange.

Question

In what ways is the disorder in the kingdom following the murder of Duncan reflected in the natural world?

MACDUFF

Is the king stirring, worthy thane?

MACBETH

        Not yet.

MACDUFF

He did command me to call timely on him: 45
I have almost slipped the hour.

MACBETH

      I'll bring you to him.

MACDUFF

I know this is a joyful trouble to you;
But yet 't is one.

MACBETH

   The labour we delight in physics pain.
This is the door.

MACDUFF

     I'll make so bold to call.
For 't is my limited service.   50

             Exit

LENOX

Goes the king hence today?

MACBETH

     He does: – he did appoint so.

LENOX

The night has been unruly: where we lay,
Our chimneys were blown down; and, as they say,
Lamentings heard i' the air; strange screams of
  death,
And prophesying with accents terrible   55

56   *dire combustion:* dreadful civil war.
      confused: disorderly.
57   *New hatched:* newly born.
      woeful: unhappy.
      obscure bird: bird of darkness, the owl.
58   *the livelong night:* all night long.
59   *shake:* with earthquake.
60   *young remembrance:* youthful memory.
60–1 *parallel . . . to it:* recall another like it.
64   *Confusion:* utter ruin, chaos.
65–6 *Most sacrilegious . . . temple:* the King was God's representative on earth: to kill him was therefore a violation of the divine order ('sacrilegious'). His body, 'anointed' with oil at his coronation, is described as a 'temple' which houses the spirit of God.
70   *Gorgon:* Medusa, the monster in Greek mythology who turned anyone who looked at her to stone. The sight of Duncan's body will, Macduff suggests, literally petrify his followers.

Question

How does the imagery used on this page highlight the enormity and the gravity of Macbeth's crime?

Of dire combustion, and confused events,
New hatched to the woeful time. The obscure bird
Clamoured the livelong night: some say the earth
Was feverous, and did shake.

MACBETH

           'T was a rough night.

LENOX

My young remembrance cannot parallel   60
A fellow to it.

Re-enter MACDUFF.

MACDUFF

O horror! horror! horror! Tongue, nor heart,
Cannot conceive, nor name thee!

MACBETH *and* LENOX

                What's the matter?

MACDUFF

Confusion now hath made his masterpiece!
Most sacrilegious murder hath broke ope   65
The Lord's anointed temple, and stole thence
The life o' the building!

MACBETH

           What is 't you say? the life?

LENOX

Mean you his majesty?

MACDUFF

Approach the chamber, and destroy your sight
With a new Gorgon. – Do not bid me speak: 70
See, and then speak yourselves. –

                Exeunt MACBETH *and* LENOX

74 *counterfeit:* imitation.
76 *The great doom's image:* a picture of Judgement Day.
77 *As from . . . like sprites:* rise from your beds as the souls of the dead will
   rise from their graves on Judgement Day, and make your way like spirits.
78 *countenance:* face.
80 *parley:* discussion between opposing forces in a battle. The bell reminds
   her of a military trumpet call.
83 *repetition:* narration.
84 *Would murder as it fell:* would kill her as she heard it.

Question

Imagine that you were directing the exchange between Lady Macbeth
and Banquo at line 86 ('What . . . anywhere'). How would you ask
the actress and actor to approach these words?

Awake! awake! –
Ring the alarum-bell. – Murder and treason!
Banquo and Donalbain! Malcolm! awake!
Shake off this downy sleep, death's counterfeit,
And look on death itself! – up, up, and see   75
The great doom's image! – Malcolm! Banquo!
As from your graves rise up, and walk like sprites
To countenance this horror! Ring the bell.

Bell rings.

Enter LADY MACBETH.

LADY MACBETH
What's the business,
That such a hideous trumpet calls to parley   80
The sleepers of the house? speak, speak!

MACDUFF
O gentle lady,
'T is not for you to hear what I can speak:
The repetition, in a woman's ear,
Would murder as it fell.

Enter BANQUO.

O Banquo! Banquo!
Our royal master's murdered!

LADY MACBETH
Woe, alas!   85
What! in our house?

BANQUO
Too cruel anywhere.
Dear Duff, I pr'ythee, contradict thyself,
And say it is not so.

Re-enter MACBETH *and* LENOX.

89   *chance:* unexpected misfortune.
91   *serious:* important.
     mortality: human life.
92   *toys:* triviality.
     renown: high distinction.
93   *drawn:* drawn off
     the mere lees: only the dregs.
94   *Is left:* remains for
     vault: The earth, vaulted by the roof of the heavens. The image also
     suggests both a wine cellar and a crypt.
     brag of: boast about.
96   *head:* fountain head.
100   *badged:* marked, as with a badge worn by servants to identify their
     masters or their craft.
103   *They started and were distracted:* this reaction could be through horror at
     the crime, or the after-effects of Lady Macbeth's drug.
106   *Wherefore:* why?

Questions

1 Explain the image at lines 93–4 ('The wine . . . brag of').
2 Why do you think Macbeth has killed the sleeping grooms?

MACBETH

    Had I but died an hour before this chance,
    I had lived a blessed time; for, from this instant,   90
    There's nothing serious in mortality;
    All is but toys: renown, and grace, is dead;
    The wine of life is drawn, and the mere lees
    Is left this vault to brag of.

Enter MALCOLM *and* DONALBAIN.

DONALBAIN

    What is amiss?

MACBETH

             You are, and do not know 't: 95
    The spring, the head, the fountain of your blood
    Is stopped; the very source of it is stopped.

MACDUFF

    Your royal father's murdered.

MALCOLM

                O! by whom?

LENOX

    Those of his chamber, as it seemed, had done 't:
    Their hands and faces were all badged with blood; 100
    So were their daggers, which, unwiped, we found
    Upon their pillows:
    They stared, and were distracted; no man's life
    Was to be trusted with them.

MACBETH

    O! yet I do repent me of my fury   105
    That I did kill them.

MACDUFF

             Wherefore did you so?

107   *amazed:* bewildered.

      temperate: self-restrained.

109–10   *The expedition . . . pauser reason:* my passionate love prompted me to move hastily, before reason could tell me to pause and think.

111   *laced:* embroidered, as if with golden thread.

112   *breach in nature:* as if nature itself had been wounded by the stabbing of the King.

113   *ruin:* death.

      wasteful: destructive.

114   *Steeped:* dyed.

      colours of their trade: livery worn by members of a trade guild. In this case the trade is murder, and the livery is blood.

115   *Unmannerly breeched:* indecently clothed.

117   *make's:* make his.

118   *Look to:* look after.

118–19   *Why do we . . . for ours?:* why are we silent, who (as the bereaved sons) have the most interest in the subject under discussion?

121   *auger-hole:* a tiny hole, made by a carpenter's boring device – with perhaps also an allusion to the hole made by the dagger.

123   *brewed:* ready to be poured out.

124   *Upon the foot of motion:* ready to be expressed.

Questions

1 In what ways does the language of Macbeth's first speech on this page suggest that he is not being sincere?

2 Why does Lady Macbeth faint? Do you believe her faint to be genuine?

MACBETH

Who can be wise, amazed, temperate and furious,
Loyal and neutral, in a moment? No man:
The expedition of my violent love
Outran the pauser reason. – Here lay Duncan,   110
His silver skin laced with his golden blood;
And his gashed stabs looked like a breach in nature
For ruin's wasteful entrance: there, the murderers,
Steeped in the colours of their trade, their daggers
Unmannerly breached with gore. Who could re-
   frain,   115
That had a heart to love, and in that heart
Courage, to make's love known?

LADY MACBETH
                    (*Fainting*) Help me hence, ho!

MACDUFF

Look to the lady.

MALCOLM

(*Aside to* DONALBAIN) Why do we hold our tongues,
That most may claim this argument for ours?

DONALBAIN

(*Aside to* MALCOLM) What should be spoken   120
Here where our fate, hid in an auger-hole,
May rush and seize us? Let's away: our tears
Are not yet brewed.

MALCOLM

(*Aside to* DONALBAIN) Nor our strong sorrow
Upon the foot of motion.

BANQUO
                        Look to the lady: –

LADY MACBETH *is carried out*

83

125 *naked frailties hid:* covered our unclad, shivering bodies. Only Macduff and Lenox are fully dressed.
126 *suffer in exposure:* tremble in the cold.
127 *question:* inquire into.
128 *scruples:* doubts.
130 *undivulged pretence:* hidden intention.
131 *treasonous malice:* treasonable wickedness.
132 *briefly:* quickly.
134 *consort:* mix.
135 *show:* pretend.
     office: task.
139–40 *the near ... bloody:* the closer our relationship, the more likely we are to get stabbed. Donalbain could either mean their relationship to the dead King or their relationship to his murderer.
140 *shaft:* arrow.
141 *lighted:* landed, hit its mark.
142 *avoid the aim:* get out of the line of fire.

Questions

1 What evidence do you find in this scene to suggest that several characters are suspicious of Macbeth?
2 Explain why Malcolm and Donalbain decide to run away. Is this the right thing for them to do, in your opinion?

And when we have our naked frailties hid,   125
That suffer in exposure, let us meet,
And question this most bloody piece of work,
To know it further. Fears and scruples shake us:
In the great hand of God I stand; and thence
Against the undivulged pretence I fight   130
Of treasonous malice.

MACDUFF

               And so do I.

ALL

                    So all.

MACBETH

Let's briefly put on manly readiness,
And meet i' the hall together.

ALL

                 Well contented.

Exeunt all but MALCOLM *and* DONALBAIN

MALCOLM

What will you do? Let's not consort with them:
To show an unfelt sorrow is an office   135
Which the false man does easy. I'll to England.

DONALBAIN

To Ireland, I: our separated fortune
Shall keep us both the safer; where we are
There's daggers in men's smiles; the near in blood,
The nearer bloody.

MALCOLM

          This murderous shaft that's shot 140
Hath not yet lighted, and our safest way
Is to avoid the aim: therefore, to horse,

143 *dainty of leave-taking:* fussy about saying good-bye.
144 *shift:* slip.
    warrant: justification.
    theft: removal of one's self – punning on 'steal away'.

1 *Threescore and ten:* seventy (years).
2 *volume:* space.
3 *sore:* dreadful.
4 *trifled former knowings:* made previous experiences seem trivial.
    good father: a normal way of addressing an older man respectfully. Rosse and the Old Man are not related.
5 *heavens:* sky.
    troubled with: disturbed by.
6 *his bloody stage:* the earth, scene of bloodshed. This image of the stage is heralded by line 5: 'The heavens' was also the name given to the canopy, painted with signs of the zodiac, which extended over the stage.
7 *travelling lamp:* the sun, which journeys across the sky.
8 *predominance:* superior influence (an astrological term).
    the day's shame: the day hiding with shame, rather than face the murder.
12 *towering:* flying very high.
    pride of place: highest pitch, before stooping on her quarry.
13 *mousing owl:* an owl that catches mice, and normally hunts close to the ground.

Questions

1 What is unusual about the day-time sky?
2 What is the effect of the word 'strangles' at line 7?

And let us not be dainty of leave-taking,
But shift away. There's warrant in that theft
Which steals itself, when there's no mercy left.   145

                                        Exeunt

Scene four

Outside the Castle.

Enter ROSSE *and an* OLD MAN.

OLD MAN

Threescore and ten I can remember well;
Within the volume of which time I have seen
Hours dreadful and things strange, but this sore
   night
Hath trifled former knowings.

ROSSE

                          Ha, good father,
Thou seest, the heavens, as troubled with man's act,   5
Threatens his bloody stage: by the clock 't is day,
And yet dark night strangles the travelling làmp.
Is 't night's predominance, or the day's shame,
That darkness does the face of earth entomb,
When living light should kiss it?

OLD MAN

                          'T is unnatural,   10
Even like the deed that's done. On Tuesday last,
A falcon, towering in her pride of place,
Was by a mousing owl hawked at, and killed.

ROSSE

And Duncan's horses (a thing most strange and
   certain)

87

15 *minions of their race:* choicest thoroughbreds.
16 *Turned wild in nature:* became like wild beasts.
17 *Contending 'gainst obedience:* rebelling against their obedience to man.
23 *Those that:* the men whom (i.e., the grooms).
24 *pretend:* aim at.
    suborned: bribed.
27 *'Gainst nature still:* unnaturalness again!
28 *Thriftless:* wasteful.
    ravin: devour.

Question

What examples of unnaturalness are described in this scene? What is the significance of this emphasis on disorder and abnormality?

Beauteous and swift, the minions of their race,   15
Turned wild in nature, broke their stalls, flung out,
Contending 'gainst obedience, as they would make
War with mankind.

OLD MAN
                    'T is said, they ate each other.

ROSSE
They did so, to th' amazement of mine eyes,
That looked upon 't –

Enter MACDUFF.

                    Here comes the good Macduff. – 20
How goes the world, Sir, now?

MACDUFF
                              Why, see you not?

ROSSE
Is 't known, who did this more than bloody deed?

MACDUFF
Those that Macbeth hath slain.

ROSSE
                              Alas, the day!
What good could they pretend?

MACDUFF
                    They were suborned.
Malcolm and Donalbain, the king's two sons,   25
Are stol'n away and fled; which puts upon them
Suspicion of the deed.

ROSSE
            'Gainst nature still:
Thriftless Ambition, that wilt ravin up

89

29 *Thine own life's means:* the source of your own life.
   like: probable.
31 *named:* elected successor.
   Scone: the ancient capital of Scotland, where its kings were crowned.
33 *Colme-kill:* Iona, the island of St Columba, where the Scottish kings were
   buried.
36 *Fife:* Macduff is going home to his own castle. He is Thane of Fife.
   thither: to Scone.
38 *Lest our old robes ... new:* in case the old reign may prove to have been
   more comfortable for Scotland than the new reign. Perhaps the image of
   clothing comes from the royal robes worn at the investiture.
40 *benison:* blessing.

Questions

1 What details show us that Macduff is uneasy about Macbeth's
  succession?
2 What general impression have you formed of Macduff from what
  he has said and done in Act 2?

Thine own life's means! – Then 't is most like
The sovereignty will fall upon Macbeth.   30

MACDUFF
He is already named, and gone to Scone
To be invested.

ROSSE
                              Where is Duncan's body?

MACDUFF
Carried to Colme-kill,
The sacred storehouse of his predecessors,
And guardian of their bones.

ROSSE
                              Will you to Scone?   35

MACDUFF
No, cousin; I'll to Fife.

ROSSE
                              Well, I will thither.

MACDUFF
Well, may you see things well done there: – adieu! –
Lest our old robes sit easier than our new!

ROSSE
Farewell, father.

OLD MAN
God's benison go with you; and with those   40
That would make good of bad, and friends of foes!

                                        Exeunt

MACBETH

1 *it:* the succession.
4 *should not . . . posterity:* would not remain with your descendants.
6 *them:* the witches.
7 *shine:* show favour, speak the truth.
8 *verities on thee made good:* things that have come true for you.
9 *my oracles:* prophets for me.
10 *Sennet:* trumpet-call, announcing a ceremonial entry.
13 *all-thing unbecoming:* altogether inappropriate.
14 *solemn:* formal.
15 *I'll:* Macbeth is no longer using the plural 'we', in order to make the invitation more friendly and personal.

Questions

1 Which line shows that Banquo suspects Macbeth of murdering Duncan?
2 Why do you think Banquo does not expose Macbeth's wickedness?

Act Three

Scene one

Forres. A room in the palace.

Enter BANQUO.

BANQUO
Thou hast it now, King, Cawdor, Glamis, all,
As the weird women promised; and, I fear,
Thou playedst most foully for 't; yet it was said,
It should not stand in thy posterity;
But that myself should be the root and father   5
Of many kings. If there come truth from them
(As upon theè, Macbeth, their speeches shine),
Why, by the verities on thee made good,
May they not be my oracles as well,
And set me up in hope? But, hush; no more.   10

Sennet sounded. Enter MACBETH *as King;* LADY MACBETH *as Queen;* LENOX, ROSSE, LORDS, *and* ATTENDANTS.

MACBETH
Here's our chief guest.

LADY MACBETH
                              If he had been forgotten,
It had been as a gap in our great feast,
And all-thing unbecoming.

MACBETH
(*To* BANQUO) Tonight we hold a solemn supper, Sir,
And I'll request your presence.

BANQUO
                              Let your highness   15

16 *Command:* give an order (as opposed to request).
    the which: your command.
17 *indissoluble tie:* tie that cannot be broken.
18 *knit:* bound.
20 *else:* otherwise.
21 *Which still . . . prosperous:* which has always been weighty and profitable.
22 *we'll take tomorrow;* we'll use tomorrow instead.
25 *this:* now.
    go not . . . the better: if my horse does not go faster than usual.
26 *become . . . night:* use one or two hours of darkness to complete the ride.
27 *Fail not:* do not fail to attend.
29 *bloody cousins:* murderous relations (Malcolm and Donalbain).
    bestowed: settled.
31 *parricide:* murder of their father.
32 *strange invention:* ridiculous stories (presumably accusing Macbeth of murder).
33 *therewithal:* in addition.
    cause: affairs.
34 *Craving us jointly:* demanding the attention of both of us.

Questions

1 In what tone of voice do you think Macbeth asks Banquo about his plans for the afternoon and early evening?
2 Why do you think he wants this information?

Command upon me, to the which my duties
Are with a most indissoluble tie
For ever knit.

MACBETH
Ride you this afternoon?

BANQUO
                              Ay, my good lord.

MACBETH
We should have else desired your good advice   20
(Which still hath been both grave and prosperous)
In this day's council; but we'll take tomorrow.
Is 't far you ride?

BANQUO
As far, my lord, as will fill up the time
'Twixt this and supper: go not my horse the better, 25
I must become a borrower of the night
For a dark hour or twain.

MACBETH
                              Fail not our feast.

BANQUO
My lord, I will not.

MACBETH
We hear our bloody cousins are bestowed
In England and in Ireland; not confessing   30
Their cruel parricide, filling their hearers
With strange invention. But of that tomorrow,
When, therewithal, we shall have cause of state
Craving us jointly. Hie you to horse; adieu,
Till you return at night. Goes Fleance with you?   35

36   *our time . . . upon 's:* it's time for us to go.
38   *commend:* entrust.
40   *master of his time:* use the time as he wishes.
41–2 *to make . . . welcome:* so that company will be especially welcome.
43   *while:* until.
44   *Sirrah:* a term used to summon or address servants.
44–5 *attend . . . our pleasure:* are those men waiting for when I'm ready to see them?
46   *without:* outside.
47   *thus:* a King.
49   *Stick:* penetrate (like daggers).
      royalty of nature: natural goodness and dignity. He has a kingly quality.
50   *would:* should.
      't is much he dares: he is courageous.
51   *to:* in addition to.
      temper: quality.
52   *wisdom:* discretion.
54   *being:* existence.
55   *My genius is rebuked:* my guardian spirit is restrained.

Question

Looking carefully at the language of Macbeth's two speeches on this page, what differences do you see between his public self and his private self?

BANQUO

Ay, my good lord: our time does call upon 's.

MACBETH

I wish your horses swift, and sure of foot;
And so I do commend you to their backs.
Farewell. –

Exit BANQUO

(*To the Lords*) Let every man be master of his time   40
Till seven at night; to make society
The sweeter welcome, we will keep ourself
Till supper-time alone: while then, God be with
you.

Exeunt LADY MACBETH, LORDS, *etc.*

(*To an* ATTENDANT) Sirrah, a word with you. Attend
those men
Our pleasure?   45

ATTENDANT

They are, my lord, without the palace gate.

MACBETH

Bring them before us. (*Exit* Attendant) – To be thus
is nothing,
But to be safely thus. – Our fears in Banquo
Stick deep, and in his royalty of nature
Reigns that which would be feared; 't is much he
dares;   50
And, to that dauntless temper of his mind,
He hath a wisdom that doth guide his valour
To act in safety. There is none but he
Whose being I do fear; and under him
My genius is rebuked, as, it is said,   55

56 *Mark Antony's was by Caesar:* Shakespeare's next tragedy, *Antony and Cleopatra*, includes a soothsayer's remark that Mark Antony's good angel fears that of Octavius Caesar (Act 2, Scene 3, lines 20–1).
   chid: reproached.
60 *fruitless:* sterile, without offspring.
61 *sceptre:* staff symbolizing royal authority.
   gripe: grasp.
62 *Thence:* from there.
   with: by.
   unlineal: not from my family line.
64 *issue:* children.
   filed: defiled.
66 *rancours:* bitterness.
   vessel: cup
   peace: peace of mind.
67 *eternal jewel:* immortal soul.
68 *common enemy of man:* devil.
70 *into the list:* to the tournament field. Macbeth is defying fate by trying to frustrate the prophecy about Banquo's sons becoming kings.
71 *champion:* fight against.
   to the utterance: to the death.
   Who's there?: a formula for summoning servants, common in Shakespeare's day.
76 *he:* Banquo.
   which: who.
77 *under fortune:* below what you deserved.
   which, you thought, had been: when you thought the culprit was.
78 *made good:* proved.
79 *conference:* conversation, meeting.
   passed in probation: went over the proofs.

Question

What reason does Macbeth give in this soliloquy for wishing Banquo dead?

Mark Antony's was by Caesar. He chid the sisters
When first they put the name of king upon me,
And bade them speak to him; then, prophet-like,
They hailed him father to a line of kings.
Upon my head they placed a fruitless crown,   60
And put a barren sceptre in my gripe,
Thence to be wrenched with an unlineal hand,
No son of mine succeeding. If 't be so,
For Banquo's issue have I filed my mind;
For them the gracious Duncan have I murdered;   65
Put rancours in the vessel of my peace
Only for them; and mine eternal jewel
Given to the common enemy of man,
To make them kings, the seed of Banquo kings!
Rather than so, come, fate, into the list,   70
And champion me to the utterance! – Who's there? –

Re-enter ATTENDANT, *with two* MURDERERS.

(*To the* ATTENDANT) Now, go to the door, and stay
    there till we call.

                                    Exit ATTENDANT

(*To the* MURDERERS) Was it not yesterday we spoke
    together?

1 MURDERER
It was, so please your highness.

MACBETH
                            Well then, now
Have you considered of my speeches? Know   75
That it was he, in the times past, which held you
So under fortune, which, you thought, had been
Our innocent self. This I made good to you
In our last conference; passed in probation with you

99

80 *borne in hand:* deceived.
    crossed: thwarted.
    the instruments: the means used.
81 *wrought with:* used.
    all things else: all other details.
82–3 *To half . . . Banquo:* convince even a half-witted idiot that Banquo did this.
85 *Our point of:* the point of our.
86 *so predominant:* such a controlling force.
87 *gospelled:* influenced by the Gospels (which advocate forgiveness of enemies).
89 *bowed:* oppressed.
90 *beggared yours:* made your children paupers.
91 *catalogue:* list.
93 *Shoughs:* shaggy dogs.
    water-rugs: rough water-dogs.
    demi-wolves: cross-breeds.
    clept: called.
94 *valued file:* graded list (ranking their individual qualities).
96 *housekeeper:* watchdog.
98 *closed:* set, like a jewel.
99 *Particular addition:* a distinguishing quality.
99–100 *the bill . . . all alike:* the catalogue that calls them all 'dogs'.
100 *so of men:* the same is true of men.
101 *station in the file:* place in the list.
102 *Not . . . manhood:* that sets you above the lowest type of person possible.
    say: prove (by your actions).

Questions

1 How does Macbeth try to justify the killing of Banquo to the murderers?
2 Why do you think Macbeth is talking so much?

How you were borne in hand; how crossed, the
    instruments;   80
Who wrought with them; and all things else, that
    might
To half a soul, and to a notion crazed,
Say, "Thus did Banquo".

1 MURDERER
                       You made it known to us.

MACBETH
I did so; and went further, which is now
Our point of second meeting. Do you find   85
Your patience so predominant in your nature
That you can let this go? Are you so gospelled
To pray for this good man, and for his issue,
Whose heavy hand hath bowed you to the grave
And beggared yours for ever?

1 MURDERER
                   We are men, my liege. 90

MACBETH
Ay, in the catalogue ye go for men;
As hounds and greyhounds, mongrels, spaniels,
    curs,
Shoughs, water-rugs, and demi-wolves are clept
All by the name of dogs: the valued file
Distinguishes the swift, the slow, the subtle, 95
The housekeeper, the hunter, every one
According to the gift which bounteous nature
Hath in him closed; whereby he does receive
Particular addition, from the bill
That writes them all alike; and so of men. 100
Now, if you have a station in the file,
Not i' the worst rank of manhood, say it;

103–4 *put that . . . enemy off:* tell you a secret plan, the carrying out of which will dispose of your enemy.
105 *Grapples:* binds.
106–7 *Who wear . . . were perfect:* whose spirit is afflicted while he lives, but would be in perfect health if he were dead.
109 *incensed:* angered.
111 *tugged with:* dragged about by.
112 *set . . . chance:* risk my life for any opportunity.
113 *mend:* improve.
115 *in such bloody distance:* so dangerously close to me ('distance' is a technical term for the space between two fencers) or to such a dangerous extent.
116 *being:* life.
116–7 *thrusts . . . of life:* threatens my own life like a sword.
118 *bare-faced:* undisguised.
119 *bid my will avouch it:* justify it simply by declaring that it was my wish.
120 *For:* because of.
121 *Whose loves I may not drop:* whose affection I must not lose.
     wail his fall: must lament his death.
122 *thence:* that is why.
123 *to your assistance do make love:* approach you for your help.
124 *Masking:* concealing.
     common: public.
125 *sundry:* many and various.

Question

What excuse does Macbeth give for not having Banquo executed publicly?

And I will put that business in your bosoms,
Whose execution takes your enemy off,
Grapples you to the heart and love of us,   105
Who wear our health but sickly in his life,
Which in his death were perfect.

2 MURDERER

                I am one, my liege.
Whom the vile blows and buffets of the world
Have so incensed, that I am reckless what
I do to spite the world.

1 MURDERER

              And I another,   110
So weary with disasters, tugged with fortune,
That I would set my life on any chance
To mend it or be rid on 't.

MACBETH

            Both of you
Know Banquo was your enemy.

BOTH MURDERERS

               True, my lord.

MACBETH

So is he mine; and in such bloody distance   115
That every minute of his being thrusts
Against my near'st of life; and though I could
With bare-faced power sweep him from my sight,
And bid my will avouch it, yet I must not,
For certain friends, that are both his and mine,   120
Whose loves I may not drop, but wail his fall
Who I myself struck down: and thence it is
That I to your assistance do make love,
Masking the business from the common eye,
For sundry weighty reasons.

127 *Your spirits . . . you:* your courage is obvious.
128 *plant:* position.
129 *Acquaint . . . o' the time:* tell you precisely the ideal time to do it.
130 *on 't:* of the murder.
131 *something:* some distance.
     always thought: always bearing in mind.
132 *I require a clearness:* I need to be kept free of suspicion.
133 *rubs:* roughnesses.
     botches: bunglings.
135 *material:* important.
137 *Resolve yourselves apart:* make up your minds in private.
139 *I'll call . . . straight:* I'll join you straight away.

Question

What similarities and differences do you see between Macbeth's approach to the murder of Duncan and his approach to this killing?

2 MURDERER

                We shall, my lord,   125
Perform what you command us.

1 MURDERER

                    Though our lives –

MACBETH

Your spirits shine through you. Within this hour at
   most
I will advise you where to plant yourselves,
Acquaint you with the perfect spy o' the time,
The moment on 't, for 't must be done tonight   130
And something from the palace; always thought
That I require a clearness: and with him
(To leave no rubs, nor botches, in the work),
Fleance his son, that keeps him company,
Whose absence is no less material to me   135
Than is his father's, must embrace the fate
Of that dark hour. Resolve yourselves apart;
I'll come to you anon.

2 MURDERER

             We are resolved, my lord.

MACBETH

I'll call upon you straight: abide within. –

Exeunt MURDERERS

It is concluded: Banquo, thy soul's flight,   140
If it find heaven, must find it out tonight.

Exit

3   *I would attend his leisure:* I would like to see him when he is free.

4–5 *Nought's . . . without content:* nothing is gained, everything is wasted, when we achieve what we want but it does not make us happy.

6   *that which we destroy:* our dead victim.

7   *doubtful:* uncertain, full of doubts and suspicions.

8   *keep alone:* stay apart from me.

9   *sorriest fancies:* saddest thoughts.

10   *Using:* being familiar with.

11   *With them they think on:* with the people whose deaths you are brooding over.

     without all remedy: that cannot be changed or mended.

12   *without regard:* ignored, unheeded.

13   *scotched:* slashed, wounded.

Question

What details show you that Lady Macbeth is feeling isolated and anxious?

Scene two

The same. Another room.

Enter LADY MACBETH *and a* SERVANT.

LADY MACBETH

  Is Banquo gone from court?

SERVANT

  Ay, Madam, but returns again tonight.

LADY MACBETH

  Say to the king, I would attend his leisure
  For a few words.

SERVANT

             Madam, I will.

                                 Exit

LADY MACBETH

                Nought's had, all's spent,
  Where our desire is got without content: 5
  'T is safer to be that which we destroy,
  Than by destruction dwell in doubtful joy.

Enter MACBETH.

  How now, my lord? Why do you keep alone,
  Of sorriest fancies your companions making,
  Using those thoughts which should indeed have
    died   10
  With them they think on? Things without all
    remedy
  Should be without regard: what's done is done.

MACBETH

  We have scotched the snake, not killed it:

14 *close:* heal.
    be herself: go back to normal, become poisonous again.
    poor malice: ineffective evil.
15 *former tooth:* the power she had before to harm us.
16 *let ... suffer:* let the structure of the universe break in pieces, afflicting both heaven and hell.
17 *Ere:* before.
20 *Whom we ... to peace:* whom we put to death in order to satisfy our own peace of mind.
21 *lie:* as on a torturing rack.
22 *ecstasy:* frenzy.
23 *fitful:* full of fits, with sudden spasms of energy.
24 *nor ... nor:* neither ...nor.
25 *Malice domestic:* hostility in his own kingdom.
    foreign levy: armies raised abroad.
27 *sleek o'er:* smooth over.
    rugged: haggard.
30 *Let ... Banquo:* remember to give special consideration to Banquo.
31 *Present him eminence:* treat him as guest of honour.
    with eye and tongue: in how you look at him and what you say.
32–3 *Unsafe ... flattering streams:* we are not safe at present, so we must keep our honour washed in these streams of flattery – that is, establish a 'pure' reputation of our courtesy to others.
34 *vizards:* masks.
35 *leave this:* stop thinking in this way.

Questions

1 Why does Macbeth feel that Duncan is in a happier position than he himself?
2 What does Macbeth mean by 'O! full of scorpions is my mind, dear wife!' (line 36)?

She'll close and be herself; whilst our poor malice
Remains in danger of her former tooth. 15
But let the frame of things disjoint, both the worlds
   suffer,
Ere we will eat our meal in fear, and sleep
In the affliction of these terrible dreams
That shake us nightly. Better be with the dead
Whom we, to gain our place, have sent to peace, 20
Than on the torture of the mind to lie
In restless ecstasy. Duncan is in his grave;
After life's fitful fever he sleeps well;
Treason has done his worst: nor steel, nor poison,
Malice domestic, foreign levy, nothing 25
Can touch him further.

LADY MACBETH

            Come on;
Gentle my lord, sleek o'er your rugged looks;
Be bright and jovial among your guests tonight.

MACBETH

So shall I, love; and so, I pray, be you.
Let your remembrance apply to Banquo: 30
Present him eminence, both with eye and tongue:
Unsafe the while, that we
Must lave our honours in these flattering streams,
And make our faces vizards to our hearts,
Disguising what they are.

LADY MACBETH

                You must leave this. 35

MACBETH

O! full of scorpions is my mind, dear wife!
Thou know'st that Banquo and his Fleance lives.

38 *in them . . . eterne:* nature has not given them an eternal lease of life.
39 *There's comfort yet:* in that there is still comfort.
    are assailable: can be attacked and defeated.
40 *jocund:* cheerful, joyful.
41 *cloistered:* furtive, secluded.
42 *shard-borne:* carried on scaly wings.
43 *yawning:* lulling the world to sleep.
    peal: curfew bell.
44 *note:* notoriety.
45 *chuck:* chick (a term of endearment).
46 *seeling:* blinding. A hawk was 'seeled' when its eyelids were sewn together
    during training in preparation for wearing a hood.
47 *Scarf up:* blindfold.
    tender: merciful.
49 *bond:* the lease of life on Banquo (and Fleance).
50 *pale:* fearful.
    crow: rook, returning to its rookery.
55 *Things bad . . . by ill:* actions begun with evil draw strength from further
    wicked deeds.

Questions

1 How does Shakespeare create an atmosphere of evil and darkness
   in Macbeth's speeches on this page?

2 What change has taken place in the relationship between husband
   and wife?

3 'Thou marvellest at my words' (line 54). How do you think Lady
   Macbeth reacts to what Macbeth is saying? Do you think she will
   be moving or still at this point?

LADY MACBETH

  But in them nature's copy's not eterne.

MACBETH

  There's comfort yet; they are assailable:
  Then be thou jocund. Ere the bat hath flown   40
  His cloistered flight; ere to black Hecate's summons
  The shard-borne beetle, with his drowsy hums,
  Hath run night's yawning peal, there shall be done
  A deed of dreadful note.

LADY MACBETH

                What's to be done?

MACBETH

  Be innocent of the knowledge, dearest chuck,   45
  Till thou applaud the deed. Come, seeling Night,
  Scarf up the tender eye of pitiful day,
  And, with thy bloody and invisible hand,
  Cancel, and tear to pieces, that great bond
  Which keeps me pale! – light thickens; and the crow 50
  Makes wing to the rooky wood;
  Good things of day begin to droop and drowse,
  Whiles night's black agents to their preys do rouse.
  Thou marvellest at my words: but hold thee still,
  Things bad begun make strong themselves by ill.   55
  So, pr'ythee, go with me.

                                 Exeunt

Scene three

The same. A park, with a road leading to the palace.

Enter three MURDERERS.

1 *who did bid thee join with us:* who told you to come along with us?
2 *He needs . . . delivers:* we need not mistrust him, since he is telling us.
3 *offices:* duties.
4 *To the direction just:* exactly as Macbeth directed.
5 *yet:* still.
6 *lated:* belated.
7 *To gain the timely inn:* to reach the welcome inn, before night falls.
8 *subject of our watch:* man we are waiting for.
9 *Give us a light:* Banquo is calling to the grooms, who will take the horses on to the palace while he and Fleance complete the journey on foot.
10 *That are . . . expectation:* that are on the list of expected guests.
11 *go about:* go the long way round.

Questions

1 Why do you think Macbeth has sent a third murderer to join the ambush of Banquo?
2 Some productions have Macbeth himself as the third murderer. What are the arguments for and against doing this?

1 MURDERER
But who did bid thee join with us?

3 MURDERER
                             Macbeth.

2 MURDERER
He needs not our mistrust, since he delivers
Our offices, and what we have to do,
To the direction just.

1 MURDERER
                   Then stand with us.
The west yet glimmers with some streaks of day: 5
Now spurs the lated traveller apace,
To gain the timely inn; and near approaches
The subject of our watch.

3 MURDERER
                    Hark, I hear horses.

BANQUO
(*Within*) Give us a light there, ho!

2 MURDERER
                       Then 't is he; the rest
That are within the note of expectation   10
Already are i' the court.

1 MURDERER
                  His horses go about.

3 MURDERER
Almost a mile, but he does usually,
So all men do, from hence to the palace gate
Make it their walk.

Enter BANQUO, *and* FLEANCE, *with a torch.*

113

15 *Stand to 't:* stand ready to act.
16 *Let it come down:* let the rain of blows fall.
20 *but:* only.

Questions

1 What do Banquo's last words show you about his character and his understanding of what has happened?

2 What does the Second Murderer mean by 'We have lost/Best half of our affair' (lines 20–1)?

2 MURDERER

A light, a light!

3 MURDERER
'T is he.

1 MURDERER

Stand to 't.   15

BANQUO
(*To* FLEANCE) It will be rain tonight.

1 MURDERER

Let it come down.

The FIRST MURDERER *strikes out the light while the others assault*
BANQUO

BANQUO
O, treachery! Fly, good Fleance, fly, fly, fly!
Thou mayest revenge – (*To the* Murderer) O slave!

Dies. FLEANCE *escapes*

3 MURDERER
Who did strike out the light?

1 MURDERER

Was 't not the way?

3 MURDERER
There's but one down: the son is fled.

2 MURDERER

We have lost   20

Best half of our affair.

1 MURDERER
Well, let's away, and say how much is done.

Exeunt

1   *degrees:* ranks. Places at table were arranged according to rank.
    at first and last: from beginning to end.
3   *society:* our guests.
5   *keeps her state:* remains seated on her throne.
    in best time: when the time is right.
6   *require her welcome:* request her to welcome you.
9   *encounter:* greet.
10 *Both sides are even:* either, now hostess and guests are equal in courtesy, or both sides of the table are equally full.
    here: at the head of the table.
11 *large:* liberal.
11–12 *we'll drink . . . round:* I'll drink a toast to the whole company.

Question

A banquet is traditionally a highly ritualistic feast, symbolizing order and harmony. What formal customs and courtesies establish an atmosphere of order at the beginning of this scene?

Scene four

A room of state in the palace. A banquet prepared.

Enter MACBETH, LADY MACBETH, ROSSE, LENOX, LORDS *and*
ATTENDANTS.

MACBETH
You know your own degrees, sit down: at first and
    last,
The hearty welcome.

LORDS
                        Thanks to your majesty.

MACBETH
Ourself will mingle with society,
And play the humble host.
Our hostess keeps her state, but in best time   5
We will require her welcome.

LADY MACBETH
Pronounce it for me, Sir, to all our friends;
For my heart speaks, they are welcome.

Enter FIRST MURDERER *to the door.*

MACBETH
    (*To* LADY MACBETH) See, they encounter thee with
        their hearts' thanks.
    (*To the Company*) Both sides are even: here I'll sit i'
        the midst.   10
Be large in mirth; anon, we'll drink a measure
The table round. (*To the* Murderer) There's blood
    upon thy face.

MURDERER
'T is Banquo's then.

117

14   *thee without . . . within:* outside you than inside him.
19   *nonpareil:* best of all.
20   *'scaped:* escaped.
21   *fit:* spasm of fear.
       else: otherwise.
22   *Whole as the marble:* firm as solid marble.
       founded: fixed, stable.
23   *As broad . . . air:* as unconfined and free as the surrounding air.
24   *cabined, cribbed:* enclosed, as in a hut or a hovel.
25   *saucy:* persistent, insolent.
       safe: dealt with.
27   *trenchèd:* deeply cut.
28   *The least . . . nature:* sufficient to kill a man.
29   *grown:* adult.
       worm: young serpent.
30   *Hath nature . . . breed:* has qualities that in time will be dangerous, as a
       snake produces venom.

Questions

1 Why does Macbeth refer to Banquo and Fleance as snakes at lines
   29–30?
2 How do you imagine the thanes and Lady Macbeth are behaving
   during Macbeth's furtive conversation with the Murderer?

MACBETH

'T is better thee without, than he within.
Is he despatched? 15

MURDERER

My lord, his throat is cut; that I did for him.

MACBETH

Thou art the best o' the cut-throats; yet he's
    good
That did the like for Fleance: if thou didst it,
Thou art the nonpareil.

MURDERER

                    Most royal Sir,
Fleance is 'scaped. 20

MACBETH

(*Aside*) Then comes my fit again: I had else been
    perfect;
Whole as the marble, founded as the rock,
As broad and general as the casing air:
But now I am cabined, cribbed, confined, bound in
To saucy doubts and fears. – (*To the* MURDERER) But
    Banquo's safe? 25

MURDERER

Ay, my good lord, safe in a ditch he bides,
With twenty trenchèd gashes on his head,
The least a death to nature.

MACBETH

                    Thanks for that. –
(*Aside*) There the grown serpent lies: the worm,
    that's fled,
Hath nature that in time will venom breed, 30

32   *hear ourselves again:* discuss the matter further.

33   *the cheer:* hospitable encouragement.

33–5 *The feast . . . welcome:* a feast is no better than a meal that has to be paid for, if the guests are not reminded frequently while it is in progress that they are welcome.

35   *To feed . . . home:* mere eating is best done at home.

36   *From thence . . . ceremony:* away from home, formal courtesies give food its special savour.

37   *Meeting:* social occasions (with a pun on 'meat').
     bare: barren.
     remembrancer: a person who reminds someone.

40–1 *Here . . . Banquo present:* all the most noble of our countrymen would be under one roof now, if only our gracious Banquo were here.

42–3 *Who may . . . mischance:* whom I hope I can rebuke for discourtesy, rather than have to pity for any accident that may have delayed him.

44   *Lays . . . promise:* makes him blameworthy, for not keeping his promise to attend.

Question

What is ironic about the timing of the Ghost's entry?

No teeth for the present. – (*To the* MURDERER) Get
    thee gone; tomorrow
We'll hear ourselves again.

Exit MURDERER

LADY MACBETH
                My royal lord,
You do not give the cheer: the feast is sold
That is not often vouched, while 't is a-making,
'T is given with welcome. To feed were best at
    home.   35
From thence, the sauce to meat is ceremony;
Meeting were bare without it.

MACBETH
                     Sweet remembrancer! –
Now, good digestion wait on appetite,
And health on both!

LENOX
              May it please your highness sit?

MACBETH
Here had we now our country's honour roofed,   40
Were the graced person of our Banquo present;

The GHOST OF BANQUO *enters, and sits in* MACBETH'S *place.*

Who may I rather challenge for unkindness,
Than pity for mischance!

ROSSE
               His absence, Sir,
Lays blame upon his promise. Please 't your high-
    ness
To grace us with your royal company?   45

49 *done this:* killed Banquo.
50 *Thou canst not say I did it:* you cannot say I killed you.
51 *gory locks:* blood-soaked hair.
53 *thus:* like this.
54 *from his youth:* since he was a child.
55 *upon a thought:* in a moment.
56 *note:* pay attention to.
57 *offend:* harm
   extend his passion: prolong the fit.

Questions

1 At what point does Macbeth become aware of the ghost?
2 Which words betray his crime?
3 How does Lady Macbeth try to explain her husband's behaviour?

MACBETH
    The table's full.

LENOX
                    Here is a place reserved, Sir.

MACBETH
    Where?

LENOX
    Here, my good lord. (MACBETH *notices the* GHOST)
        What is 't that moves your highness?

MACBETH
    Which of you have done this?

LORDS
                            What, my good lord?

MACBETH
    (*To the* GHOST) Thou canst not say I did it. Never
        shake   50
    Thy gory locks at me.

ROSSE
    Gentlemen, rise; his highness is not well.

LADY MACBETH
    Sit, worthy friends. My lord is often thus,
    And hath been from his youth: pray you, keep seat;
    The fit is momentary; upon a thought   55
    He will again be well. If much you note him
    You shall offend him, and extend his passion;
    Feed, and regard him not. – (*To* MACBETH) Are you
        a man?

MACBETH
    Ay, and a bold one, that dare look on that
    Which might appal the devil.

123

60 *proper stuff:* fine nonsense!
61 *painting:* representation, not reality.
62 *air-drawn:* imaginary; also, drawn along through the air.
63 *flaws:* outbursts.
64 *Impostors . . . fear:* not genuine, in comparison with real fear.
become: befit, suit.
66 *Authorised by her grandam:* which her grandmother said was true – an old wives' tale.
Shame itself: you are shame personified.
70 *nod:* move your head.
71 *charnel-houses:* store-houses for the bones of the dead.
72 *monuments:* tombs.
73 *maws:* stomachs. Macbeth means that if corpses will not stay buried we should allow birds of prey to eat the dead, since they would not then be able to return.
quite . . . folly?: is your manhood completely destroyed by this foolishness?
76 *Ere . . . gentle weal:* before human laws purged society of evil and so made it gentle.
78 *the time has been:* but up until now it has always been the case.

Questions

1 Can Lady Macbeth see the ghost?
2 Do you believe that the ghost is real? If not, how do you explain it?
3 In what way does line 70 ('Why, what care I?') show a change in Macbeth's attitude?

LADY MACBETH

O proper stuff!   60
This is the very painting of your fear:
This is the air-drawn dagger which, you said,
Led you to Duncan. O! these flaws and starts
(Impostors to true fear) would well become
A woman's story at a winter's fire,   65
Authorised by her grandam. Shame itself!
Why do you make such faces? When all's done,
You look but on a stool.

MACBETH

(*To the* LORDS) Pr'ythee, see there! behold! look! lo!
    how say you?
Why, what care I? (*To the* GHOST) If thou canst nod,
    speak too. –
(*To the* LORDS) If charnel-houses and our graves
    must send
Those that we bury back, our monuments
Shall be the maws of kites.

GHOST *disappears*

LADY MACBETH

What! quite unmanned in folly?

MACBETH

If I stand here, I saw him.

LADY MACBETH

Fie! for shame!

MACBETH

Blood hath been shed ere now, i' th' olden time,   75
Ere humane statute purged the gentle weal;
Ay, and since too, murders have been performed
Too terrible for the ear: the time has been

81   *mortal murders:* fatal wounds.
      crowns: heads.
82-3 *more strange . . . is:* even more unnatural than Banquo's murder.
84   *lack you:* miss your company.
85   *muse:* be amazed.
86   *infirmity:* illness.
88   *Then:* when I have drunk your health.
91   *To all . . . thirst:* I long to drink to all, and to Banquo.
92   *all to all:* all good wishes all round, or all shall drink to all.
      Our duties, and the pledge: we offer our homage and drink the loyal toast.
93   *Avaunt:* go away!
95   *speculation:* power of sight or thought.

Questions

1 What makes Macbeth regain his composure?
2 Why do you think the ghost reappears?

That, when the brains were out, the man would die,
And there an end; but now they rise again,   80
With twenty mortal murders on their crowns,
And push us from our stools. This is more strange
Than such a murder is.

LADY MACBETH

                My worthy lord,
Your noble friends do lack you.

MACBETH

             (*To* LADY MACBETH) I do forget. –
(*To the* LORDS) Do not muse at me, my most worthy
   friends;   85
I have a strange infirmity, which is nothing
To those that know me. Come, love and health to
   all;
Then, I'll sit down. – Give me some wine: fill full: –
I drink to the general joy of the whole table,
And to our dear friend Banquo, whom we miss;   90
Would he were here.

Re-enter GHOST.

            To all, and him, we thirst,
And all to all.

LORDS

          Our duties, and the pledge.

MACBETH

(*To the* GHOST) Avaunt! and quit my sight! let the
   earth hide thee!
Thy bones are marrowless, thy blood is cold;
Thou hast no speculation in those eyes,   95
Which thou dost glare with.

97	*thing of custom:* normal happening.
100	*like:* in the form of.
101	*armed:* horned.
	Hyrcan: from Hyrcania, a region on the Caspian Sea.
102	*that:* the form of Banquo.
104	*dare me to the desert:* challenge me to single combat, in isolation where I can call on no assistance.
105	*trembling I inhabit:* stay at home afraid, or live in fear.
106	*baby of a girl:* a baby girl, or the child of an immature mother.
109	*diplaced:* driven away.
	mirth: merriment.
110	*admired disorder:* astounding lack of self-control.
111	*overcome:* pass over.
112	*Without our special wonder:* without causing amazement.
112–3	*You make. . . owe:* you make me doubt my own nature.
116	*blanched:* turned white.

Question

'What man dare, I dare' (line 99); 'I am a man again' (line 108).
(a) Why is 'manliness' so important to Macbeth?
(b) What other references to traditional male and female roles have been made in this scene?

LADY MACBETH

      (*To the* Lords) Think of this, good peers,
But as a thing of custom: 't is no other;
Only it spoils the pleasure of the time.

MACBETH

What man dare, I dare:
Approach thou like the rugged Russian bear,   100
The armèd rhinoceros, or the Hyrcan tiger;
Take any shape but that, and my firm nerves
Shall never tremble: or, be alive again,
And dare me to the desert with thy sword;
If trembling I inhabit then, protest me   105
The baby of a girl. Hence, horrible shadow!
Unreal mockery, hence! –

                          GHOST *disappears*

               Why, so; – being gone,
I am a man again. – Pray you, sit still.

LADY MACBETH

    (*To* MACBETH) You have displaced the mirth, broke
      the good meeting,
With most admired disorder.

MACBETH

                Can such things be,   110
And overcome us like a summer's cloud,
Without our special wonder? You make me strange
Even to the disposition that I owe,
When now I think you can behold such sights,
And keep the natural ruby of your cheeks,   115
When mine is blanched with fear.

ROSSE

                    What sights, my lord?

118 *At once:* I take leave of you all together.
119 *Stand not . . . going:* do not worry about the correct procedure for leave-taking (which involves individual farewells).
122 *It will have blood:* the murder will be avenged.
123 *Stones:* gravestones (raised to reveal the body of a murder victim).
trees to speak: voices from trees have revealed murderers.
124 *Augurs:* auguries – omens read from the flight and behaviour of birds.
understood relations: the seeing of connections between signs and future actions.
125 *magot-pies:* magpies.
choughs: jackdaws. All three of the birds mentioned here are traditionally birds of ill omen. Significantly, they can also be taught to talk.
brought forth: revealed.
126 *man of blood:* murderer.
What is the night?: what time of night is it?
127 *Almost . . . which:* it is so close to morning that there could almost be a dispute between night and morning over whether it is the end of night or the beginning of day.
128 *How say'st . . . person:* what do you think of Macduff's refusal to attend?
130 *by the way:* casually.
131–2 *There's not . . . fee'd:* there is no important person in whose household I do not have a paid informer.

Question

How does the way in which the guests leave show that order has now broken down in Macbeth's kingdom?

130

LADY MACBETH

    (*To the* Lords) I pray you, speak not; he grows worse
      and worse;
    Question enrages him. At once, good night: –
    Stand not upon the order of your going,
    But go at once.

LENOX

                Good night, and better health   120
    Attend his majesty!

LADY MACBETH

              A kind good night to all.

                Exeunt LORDS *and* ATTENDANTS

MACBETH

    It will have blood, they say, blood will have blood:
    Stones have been known to move, and trees to
      speak;
    Augurs, and understood relations, have
    By magot-pies and choughs, and rooks, brought
      forth   125
    The secret'st man of blood. What is the night?

LADY MACBETH

    Almost at odds with morning, which is which.

MACBETH

    How say'st thou, that Macduff denies his person
    At our great bidding?

LADY MACBETH

              Did you send to him, Sir?

MACBETH

    I hear it by the way; but I will send.   130
    There's not a one of them, but in his house

133 *betimes:* quickly, early.
134 *bent:* determined.
135 *By the worst means:* by the most evil methods.
    For mine own good: in support of my own welfare.
136 *causes:* other considerations.
137 *more:* further.
138 *go o'er:* continuing to the other side.
139 *will to hand:* will be done.
140 *Which must . . . scanned:* which must be done before they can be thought about.
141 *season of all natures:* power which preserves all life.
142–3 *My strange . . . use;* my strange self-deception is the fear of a novice in evil. It needs to be hardened by practice.
144 *young in deed:* inexperienced in action of this sort (i.e., murder)

Questions

1 How is Lady Macbeth's weariness shown in the last section of this scene?
2 What is the significance of Macbeth's decision to seek out the witches deliberately?
3 What does Macbeth mean at lines 136–8 ('I am . . . go o'er')?
4 Whom do you think Macbeth is planning to kill next?
5 Do you feel disgust, admiration or pity for Macbeth at the end of this scene?

(III.V) It is highly probable that this scene was not written by Shakespeare himself.
1 *how now:* what's the matter?
  angerly: angrily.
2 *beldams:* hags.
3 *Saucy:* presumptuous.
4 *traffic:* have dealings.

I keep a servant fee'd. I will tomorrow
(And betimes I will) to the weird sisters:
More shall they speak; for now I am bent to
    know,
By the worst means, the worst. For mine own
    good   135
All causes shall give way: I am in blood
Stepped in so far, that, should I wade no more,
Returning were as tedious as go o'er.
Strange things I have in head, that will to hand,
Which must be acted, ere they may be scanned.   140

LADY MACBETH

You lack the season of all natures, sleep.

MACBETH

Come, we'll to sleep. My strange and self-abuse
Is the initiate fear, that wants hard use:
We are yet but young in deed.

Exeunt

Scene five

The heath.

Thunder. Enter the THREE WITCHES, *meeting* HECATE.

1 WITCH

Why, how now, Hecate? you look angerly.

HECATE

Have I not reason, beldams as you are,
Saucy, and overbold? How did you dare
To trade and traffic with Macbeth,
In riddles, and affairs of death;   5

7   *close contriver:* secret plotter.
11 *wayward:* disloyal – i.e., not devoted to witchcraft.
15 *pit of Acheron:* cavern by the Acheron. Acheron was one of the rivers of Hell, according to Greek mythology.
18 *vessels:* cauldrons.
20 *for the air:* going to fly.
21 *Unto:* for.
    dismal: disastrous.
    end: purpose, result.
24 *vaporous drop profound:* very mysterious drop of vapour.
26 *sleights:* secret arts.
27 *artificial sprites:* magic apparitions.
28 *illusion:* power to deceive.
29 *confusion:* destruction.
30 *bear:* trust.
31 *'bove wisdom:* more than is wise. He will be guided by his hopes rather than by prudence.
32 *security:* over-confidence.
34 *spirit:* familiar (see Act 1, Scene 1).
35 *stays:* waits.
    Exit: traditionally, a device looking like a cloud is lowered on to the stage. Hecate then mounts it, and it re-ascends.

Questions

1 Do you think Hecate's description of Macbeth at lines 11–13 is accurate?
2 If Shakespeare did *not* write this scene, why do you think it has been inserted?

And I, the mistress of your charms,
The close contriver of all harms,
Was never called to bear my part,
Or show the glory of our art?
And, which is worse, all you have done   10
Hath been but for a wayward son,
Spiteful and wrathful; who, as others do,
Loves for his own ends, not for you.
But make amends now: get you gone,
And at the pit of Acheron   15
Meet me i' the morning: thither he
Will come to know his destiny.
Your vessels and your spells provide,
Your charms, and everything beside.
I am for the air; this night I'll spend   20
Unto a dismal and a fatal end:
Great business must be wrought ere noon.
Upon the corner of the moon
There hangs a vaporous drop profound;
I'll catch it ere it come to ground: 25
And that, distilled by magic sleights,
Shall raise such artificial sprites,
As, by the strength of their illusion,
Shall draw him on to his confusion.
He shall spurn fate, scorn death, and bear   30
His hopes 'bove wisdom, grace and fear;
And you all know, security
Is mortals' chiefest enemy.

Song, within: "Come away, come away," etc.

Hark! I am called: my little spirit, see,
Sits in a foggy cloud, and stays for me.   35

Exit

1 *but hit:* only hinted at.
2 *interpret farther:* deduce my meaning.
- 3 *strangely borne:* carried out in an odd way.
4 *of:* by.
  marry, he was dead: but of course, he was dead. To pity the dead is easy enough.
6 *you may . . . killed:* you might choose to believe was killed by Fleance.
7 *For:* since.
  Men must not walk too late: it is foolish to be out late at night. The tone of these remarks is obviously very ironic.
8 *cannot want the thought:* can fail to think.
  monstrous: unnatural.
10 *fact:* deed.
11 *straight:* immediately.
12 *pious:* loyal, religious.
  delinquents: the grooms who had failed in their duty.
  tear: stab.
13 *thralls:* captives.
17 *borne all things well:* responded admirably to everything.
18 *under his key:* in his power.
19 *an 't:* if it.
19–20 *should find . . . father:* would find out what it is really like to kill one's father. Macbeth would execute them.

Question

How is Lenox's contempt for Macbeth made clear in this speech?

1 WITCH
>Come, let's make haste: she'll soon be back
>again.

Exeunt

Scene six

Somewhere in Scotland.

Enter LENOX *and another* LORD.

LENOX
>My former speeches have but hit your thoughts,
>Which can interpret farther: only, I say,
>Things have been strangely borne. The gracious
>>Duncan
>Was pitied of Macbeth: – marry, he was dead; –
>And the right-valiant Banquo walked too late;   5
>Whom, you may say, if 't please you, Fleance
>>killed,
>For Fleance fled. Men must not walk too late.
>Who cannot want the thought how monstrous
>It was for Malcolm and for Donalbain
>To kill their gracious father? damnèd fact!   10
>How it did grieve Macbeth! did he not straight,
>In pious rage, the two delinquents tear,
>That were the slaves of drink, and thralls of sleep?
>Was not that nobly done? Ay, and wisely, too;
>For 't would have angered any heart alive   15
>To hear the men deny 't. So that, I say,
>He has borne all things well; and I do think
>That, had he Duncan's sons under his key.
>(As, an 't please Heaven, he shall not), they
>>should find

137

21   *for:* because.
     broad: outspoken.
21–2 *failed ... presence:* refused to appear.
24   *bestows himself:* is staying.
     son of Duncan: Malcolm.
25   *holds the due of birth:* withholds his birthright (to be King).
27   *Of:* by.
     Edward: King Edward the Confessor.
28–9 *the malevolence ... respect:* his misfortunes in no way diminish the honour shown to him.
30   *upon his aid:* in his support.
31   *wake:* arouse.
     Northumberland: the Earl of Northumberland is later called Old Siward.
     Siward: Northumberland's son, later called Young Siward.
32–3 *with Him ... the work:* with God to support the enterprise.
35   *Free from ... knives:* rid our feasts and banquets of bloody daggers.
36   *faithful:* loyal to our rightful king.
     free: honestly acquired.
37   *this report:* news from England.
38   *king:* Macbeth.
40–1 *with ... his back:* being met with a flat refusal, the sullen messenger turned away.
42   *hums, as who should say:* muttered, as if he were saying.
     rue: regret.
43   *clogs:* burdens.

Question

At line 34, the Lord says that it is no longer possible to eat and sleep properly in the kingdom. Explain in detail the significance of food and sleep in *Macbeth* so far.

What 't were to kill a father; so should Fleance.   20
But, peace! – for from broad words, and 'cause he
      failed
His presence at the tyrant's feast, I hear
Macduff lives in disgrace. Sir, can you tell
Where he bestows himself?

LORD

                The son of Duncan,
From whom this tyrant holds the due of birth,   25
Lives in the English court; and is received
Of the most pious Edward with such grace,
That the malevolence of fortune nothing
Takes from his high respect. Thither Macduff
Is gone to pray the holy king, upon his aid,   30
To wake Northumberland, and warlike Siward;
That, by the help of these (with Him above
To ratify the work), we may again
Give to our tables meat, sleep to our nights,
Free from our feasts and banquets bloody knives.   35
Do faithful homage, and receive free honours,
All which we pine for now. And this report
Hath so exasperate the king that he
Prepares for some attempt of war.

LENOX

                Sent he to Macduff?

LORD

He did: and with an absolute "Sir, not I,"   40
The cloudy messenger turns me his back,
And hums, as who should say, "You'll rue the time
That clogs me with this answer."

LENOX

                And that well might

44–5 *hold what . . . provide:* stay as far away as he has sense to.
  47 *His:* Macduff's.
48–9 *our . . . Under:* our country, suffering under.

Questions

1 What is the effect of the religious imagery in this speech?
2 In what ways has Act 3 proved to be a turning-point in the play?

Advise him to a caution, to hold what distance
His wisdom can provide. Some holy angel   45
Fly to the court of England, and unfold
His message ere he come, that a swift blessing
May soon return to this our suffering country
Under a hand accursed!

LORD

        I'll send my prayers with him.

Exeunt

MACBETH

1   *brinded:* streaked, tabby.
2   *hedge-pig:* hedgehog.
3   *Harpier:* the third Witch's familiar (possibly some form of bird).
5   *poisoned entrails:* organs torn from poisonous animals.
8   *Sweltered venom:* sweated-out poison.
     sleeping got: captured in its sleep.
10 *Double . . . trouble:* Let toil and trouble in the world be doubled.
12 *Fillet . . . snake:* a slice of snakes from the fens.
16 *fork:* forked tongue.
17 *howlet:* owlet.

Question

What atmosphere is created by the rhythm and rhyme of the witches' spell?

Act Four

Scene one

A dark cave. In the middle, a boiling cauldron.

Thunder. Enter the THREE WITCHES.

1 WITCH
  Thrice the brinded cat hath mewed.

2 WITCH
  Thrice, and once the hedge-pig whined.

3 WITCH
  Harpier cries, 't is time, 't is time.

1 WITCH
  Round about the cauldron go;
  In the poisoned entrails throw.   5
  Toad, that under cold stone
  Days and nights has thirty-one
  Sweltered venom, sleeping got,
  Boil thou first i' th' charmèd pot.

ALL
  Double, double, toil and trouble: 10
  Fire, burn; and cauldron, bubble.

2 WITCH
  Fillet of a fenny snake,
  In the cauldron boil and bake;
  Eye of newt, and toe of frog,
  Wool of bat and tongue of dog,   15
  Adder's fork, and blind-worm's sting,
  Lizard's leg, and howlet's wing,
  For a charm of powerful trouble,

23 *Witches' mummy:* a body mummified by witches.
   maw, and gulf: stomach and gullet.
24 *ravined:* gorged or glutted (with fish).
25 *hemlock:* a poisonous plant.
26 *blaspheming Jew:* the Jew, like the Turk and Tartar (line 29), is not Christian, and thus considered a suitable ingredient for a pagan potion.
27 *slips of yew:* cuttings from a yew tree. Yew trees traditionally grow in graveyards and are considered poisonous.
28 *Slivered:* sliced off.
   moon's eclipse: a time of ill omen.
30 *birth-strangled:* strangled at birth, and therefore unbaptized.
31 *Ditch-delivered:* born in a ditch.
   drab: prostitute.
32 *slab:* sticky.
33 *chaudron:* entrails.
39 *commend your pains:* thank you for the trouble you have taken.

Question

Describe the contents of the witches' brew. What do the different groups of ingredients have in common?

Like a hell-broth boil and bubble.

ALL

Double, double, toil and trouble: 20
Fire, burn; and cauldron, bubble.

3 WITCH

Scale of dragon, tooth of wolf;
Witches' mummy: maw, and gulf,
Of the ravined salt-sea shark;
Root of hemlock, digged i' th' dark;   25
Liver of blaspheming Jew;
Gall of goat, and slips of yew
Slivered in the moon's eclipse;
Nose of Turk, and Tartar's lips;
Finger of birth-strangled babe,   30
Ditch-delivered by a drab,
Make the gruel thick and slab:
Add thereto a tiger's chaudron,
For th' ingredients of our cauldron.

ALL

Double, double, toil and trouble:
Fire, burn; and cauldron, bubble.   35

2 WITCH

Cool it with a baboon's blood:
Then the charm is firm and good.

Enter HECATE.

HECATE

O, well done! I commend your pains,
And every one shall share i' th' gains.   40
And now about the cauldron sing,
Like elves and fairies in a ring,
Enchanting all that you put in.

44 *pricking of my thumbs:* traditionally, itching thumbs foretell evil.
48 *black:* because they are creatures of darkness and do black magic.
49 *without a name:* too dreadful to be named.
50 *conjure:* call upon.
   by that . . . profess: by the evil magic you practise yourselves.
51 *Howe'er . . . know it:* no matter how you have acquired the knowledge –
   even if you have contacted the devil himself.
52 *Though:* even if.
   untie: let loose.
53 *yesty:* foaming.
54 *Confound:* destroy.
   navigation: shipping.
55 *bladed corn be lodged:* unripened corn be blown flat.
57 *slope:* bend.
59 *nature's germens:* the seeds of all created life.
   tumble all together: become mixed together chaotically.
60 *sicken:* becomes surfeited with disorder.

Question

How does Shakespeare make Macbeth himself seem demonic in this scene?

Music and a song, "Black spirits," etc.

2 WITCH

By the pricking of my thumbs,
Something wicked this way comes. – (*Knocking*)   45
Open, locks,
Whoever knocks.

Enter MACBETH.

MACBETH

How now, you secret, black and midnight hags!
What is 't you do?

ALL

A deed without a name.

MACBETH

I conjure you, by that which you profess,   50
Howe'er you come to know it, answer me:
Though you untie the winds, and let them fight
Against the churches, though the yesty waves
Confound and swallow navigation up;
Though bladed corn be lodged, and trees blown
    down;   55
Though castles topple on their warders' heads;
Though palaces and pyramids do slope
Their heads to their foundations; though the
    treasure
Of nature's germens tumble all together,
Even till destruction sicken, answer me   60
To what I ask you.

1 WITCH

Speak.

2 WITCH

Demand.

63 *our masters:* the evil spirits whom the witches serve (who now take the forms of the Apparitions).
65 *farrow:* litter.
    sweaten: sweated.
66 *gibbet:* gallows.
67 *high or low:* whatever your rank in the order of spirits.
68 *office:* function, task.
    armed head: head wearing a helmet.
73 *caution:* warning.
74 *harped:* judged, guessed.

Questions

1 Macbeth speaks in a casual and familiar way about the Apparitions ('Call 'em; let me see 'em'). What details show that they are far more powerful and dangerous than he thinks?
2 What is Macbeth likely to think the armed head represents?

3 WITCH

We'll answer.

1 WITCH

Say, if thou 'dst rather hear it from our mouths,
Or from our masters.

MACBETH

Call 'em; let me see 'em.

1 WITCH

Pour in sow's blood, that hath eaten
Her nine farrow, grease, that's sweaten   65
From the murderer's gibbet, throw
Into the flame.

ALL

Come, high or low,
Thyself, and office, deftly show.

Thunder. First APPARITION, *an armed head.*

MACBETH

Tell me, thou unknown power, –

1 WITCH

He knows thy thought:
Hear his speech, but say thou nought.   70

1 APPARITION

Macbeth! Macbeth! Macbeth! beware Macduff;
Beware the Thane of Fife. – Dismiss me. – Enough.

Descends

MACBETH

Whate'er thou art, for thy good caution, thanks:
Thou hast harped my fear aright. But one word
   more: –

149

78 *three ears:* that is, one for each call of his name.
84 *take a bond of fate:* take a guarantee (a legal 'bond') from fate, to ensure the prophecy comes true.
   thou: Macduff.
85 *That I . . . lies:* so that I can be certain my cowardly fears are false.
86 *in spite of thunder:* soundly, even through thunder.
87 *issue:* child.
88–9 *round/And top:* crown.
90 *lion-mettled:* lion-hearted, courageous.
   take no care: do not worry.
91 *chafes:* is angry.
   frets: complains.
   conspirers: plotters.

Questions

1 What two statements convince Macbeth that he cannot be defeated, despite the First Apparition's warning?
2 Why does Macbeth still decide to kill Macduff, even though the prophecies appear to suggest he is safe?

1 WITCH
  He will not be commanded. Here's another,   75
  More potent than the first.

Thunder. Second APPARITION, *a bloody child.*

2 APPARITION
  Macbeth! Macbeth! Macbeth! –

MACBETH
  Had I three ears, I'd hear thee.

2 APPARITION
  Be bloody, bold and resolute: laugh to scorn
  The power of man, for none of woman born   80
  Shall harm Macbeth.

                                        Descends

MACBETH
  Then live, Macduff: what need I fear of thee?
  But yet I'll make assurance double sure,
  And take a bond of fate: thou shalt not live;
  That I may tell pale-hearted Fear it lies.   85
  And sleep in spite of thunder. –

Thunder. Third APPARITION, *a child crowned, with a tree in
his hand.*

                              What is this,
  That rises like the issue of a king;
  And wears upon his baby brow the round
  And top of sovereignty?

ALL
                        Listen, but speak not to 't.

3 APPARITION
  Be lion-mettled, proud, and take no care   90
  Who chafes, who frets, or where conspirers are:

93 *Birnam . . . Dunsinane:* Birnam (a wooded hill) is twelve miles from Dunsinane.

95 *impress:* conscript into the army.

96 *bodements:* prophecies.

97 *Rebellious dead:* Banquo, and Macbeth's future victims.

99 *lease of nature:* natural length of life.

99–100 *pay . . . custom:* give up his life to old age and natural causes of death (as though returning a debt that is owed to nature).

Question

Why do you think Macbeth asks whether Banquo's children will ever reign 'in *this* kingdom' (line 103)?

Macbeth shall never vanquished be, until
Great Birnam wood to high Dunsinane hill
Shall come against him.

Descends

MACBETH

That will never be:
Who can impress the forest; bid the tree   95
Unfix his earth-bound root? Sweet bodements!
    good!
Rebellious dead, rise never, till the wood
Of Birnam rise; and our high-placed Macbeth
Shall live the lease of nature, pay his breath
To time and mortal custom. – Yet my heart   100
Throbs to know one thing: tell me (if your art
Can tell so much), shall Banquo's issue ever
Reign in this kingdom?

ALL

Seek to know no more.

MACBETH

I will be satisfied: deny me this,
And an eternal curse fall on you! let me know. –   105
Why sinks that cauldron? and what noise is this?

Hautboys.

1 WITCH
Show!

2 WITCH
Show!

3 WITCH
Show!

111   *depart:* depart in the same way.
      eight Kings: the procession consists of the eight Stuart kings, ancestors of James I. See 'Studying *Macbeth*', pages 237–8. Macbeth speaks to them in turn.

113   *sear:* scorch, brand.

114   *gold-bound:* crowned.

116   *Start:* jump from your sockets (so I can see no more).

119   *glass:* magic mirror, revealing the future.

121   *two-fold ... sceptres:* the rule of James I united the thrones of Scotland and England: 'two-fold balls' refers to orbs from both Scottish and English coronations, and 'treble sceptres' refers to the one sceptre used in the Scottish coronation rites and the two sceptres used in English coronations.

123   *blood-boltered:* with hair matted with blood.

124   *points at them for his:* indicates that they are his descendants.

126   *amazèdly:* in amazement, stupefied.

127   *sprites:* spirits.

130   *antic round:* fantastic dance in a circle.

132   *Our duties ... pay:* our homage has given him the welcome that was due to him.

Question

Imagine you were directing the whole of this scene on the stage. How would you present the three Apparitions and the procession of Kings?

ALL

    Show his eyes, and grieve his heart;   110

    Come like shadows, so depart.

A show of eight Kings, the last with a glass in his hand:
BANQUO'S GHOST *following.*

MACBETH

    (*To the first King in the show*) Thou art too like the
      spirit of Banquo: down!

    Thy crown does sear mine eye-balls: (*To the second*
      King) and thy hair,

    Thou other gold-bound brow, is like the first: –

    (*To the* WITCHES) A third is like the former: – filthy
      hags!   115

    Why do you show me this? – a fourth? – Start, eyes!

    What! will the line stretch out to th' crack of doom.

    Another yet? – A seventh? – I'll see no more: –

    And yet the eighth appears, who bears a glass

    Which shows me many more; and some I see   120

    That two-fold balls and treble sceptres carry.

    Horrible sight! – Now, I see 't is true;

    For the blood-boltered Banquo smiles upon me,

    And points at them for his. – What! is this so?

1 WITCH

    Ay, Sir, all this is so: – but why   125

    Stands Macbeth thus amazèdly?

    Come, sisters, cheer we up his sprites,

    And show the best of our delights.

    I'll charm the air to give a sound,

    While you perform your antic round;   130

    That this great king may kindly say,

    Our duties did his welcome pay.

Music. The WITCHES *dance, and vanish with* HECATE.

MACBETH

    Where are they? Gone? – Let this pernicious hour

134 *aye accursèd:* forever cursed.
135 *without there:* you outside.
138 *Infected be the air:* let the air be diseased and contaminate them.
144 *anticipat'st:* forestall.
145–6 *The flighty ... it:* your actions will never catch up with your intentions
       unless you act at once – so that the action accompanies the thought.
147 *firstlings:* firstborn.

Question

What does Macbeth mean by lines 146–8 ('From ... my hand')?

Stand aye accursèd in the calendar! –
Come in, without there!

Enter LENOX.

LENOX

What's your grace's will? 135

MACBETH

Saw you the weird sisters?

LENOX

No, my lord.

MACBETH

Came they not by you?

LENOX

No, indeed, my lord.

MACBETH

Infected be the air whereon they ride;
And damned all those that trust them! – I did hear
The galloping of horse: who was 't came by? 140

LENOX

'T is two or three, my lord, that bring you word,
Macduff is fled to England.

MACBETH

Fled to England?

LENOX

Ay, my good lord.

MACBETH

(*Aside*) Time, thou anticipat'st my dread exploits:
The flighty purpose never is o'ertook, 145
Unless the deed go with it. From this moment
The very firstlings of my heart shall be
The firstlings of my hand. And even now,

---

149 *crown:* complete.
      and done: and done at once.
150 *surprise:* take by surprise.
153 *trace him in his line:* are descended from him.
155 *sights:* apparitions.

Question

What are your feelings towards Macbeth at this stage in the play? Has your view of him altered at all during this scene?

---

1 *he:* Macduff.
3–4 *when our actions ... traitors:* even when we are not really traitors our actions can make us appear so.
7 *titles:* possessions.
9 *wants the natural touch:* lacks a father's instinct to protect his family.

To crown my thoughts with acts, be it thought and
   done:
The castle of Macduff I will surprise,   150
Seize upon Fife; give to th' edge o' th' sword
His wife, his babes, and all unfortunate souls
That trace him in his line. No boasting, like a fool;
This deed I'll do, before this purpose cool:
But no more sights! – (*To* LENOX) Where are these
   gentlemen?   155
Come, bring me where they are.

                            Exeunt

Scene two

Fife. A room in MACDUFF'S *castle.*

Enter LADY MACDUFF, *her* SON, *and* ROSSE.

LADY MACDUFF

What had he done, to make him fly the land?

ROSSE

You must have patience, madam.

LADY MACDUFF

                     He had none:
His flight was madness: when our actions do not,
Our fears do make us traitors.

ROSSE

                You know not
Whether it was his wisdom or his fear.   5

LADY MACDUFF

Wisdom! to leave his wife, to leave his babes,
His mansion, and his titles, in a place
From whence himself does fly? He loves us not;
He wants the natural touch; for the poor wren,

159

10   *most diminutive:* smallest.
12   *All . . . love:* he is acting only out of fear for himself, not love for his family.
14   *So runs against:* is so contrary.
      coz: cousin – but used as a general term for any close relationship.
15   *school:* control.
      for: as for.
16–7 *best knows . . . season:* best understands the violent way events are moving.
18   *are traitors:* are said to be traitors.
19   *know ourselves:* know that we are traitors.
19–20 *hold rumour . . . we fear:* accept rumours because we are afraid, although our fears are not specific.
21   *float . . . sea:* are tossed by troubles.
22   *Each way, and move:* in all directions, and move aimlessly.
23   *Shall:* it will.
24   *Things . . . climb upward:* when things are at their worst, they must either end completely or improve.
29   *my disgrace:* my shame (becaue he would weep).
      your discomfort: embarrassing for you.
30   *Sirrah:* used as a term of affection.
      dead: absent from our lives, dead to us.

Question

Lady Macbeth refers to 'the owl' (line 11). What references have been made to owls and other birds in the play so far? What does 'owl' symbolize here?

The most diminutive of birds, will fight,   10
Her young ones in her nest, against the owl.
All is the fear, and nothing is the love;
As little is the wisdom, where the flight
So runs against all reason.

ROSSE
                                        My dearest coz,
I pray you, school yourself: but, for your husband, 15
He is noble, wise, judicious, and best knows
The fits o' th' season. I dare not speak much
    further:
But cruel are the times, when we are traitors,
And do not know ourselves; when we hold rumour
From what we fear, yet know not what we fear,   20
But float upon a wild and violent sea
Each way, and move – I take my leave of you:
Shall not be long but I'll be here again.
Things at the worst will cease, or else climb upward
To what they were before. – (*To her* SON) My, pretty
    cousin,   25
Blessing upon you!

LADY MACDUFF
Fathered he is, and yet he's fatherless.

ROSSE
I am so much a fool, should I stay longer,
It would be my disgrace and your discomfort:
I take my leave at once.

                                                Exit

LADY MACDUFF
        (*To her* SON) Sirrah, your father's dead: 30
And what will you do now? How will you live?

161

32 *As birds do:* probably a reference to Matthew 6:26 ('Behold the fowls of the air . . . your heavenly father feedeth them').

34 *lime:* bird-lime, spread on twigs to catch birds.

35 *pit-fall:* snare.
   gin: trap.

37 *Poor birds . . . set for:* no one sets traps for poor, unimportant birds.

42 *to sell again:* because she cannot want twenty husbands.

43-4 *Thou speakest . . . for thee:* that comment stretches all your limited intelligence to the full – although you are quite intelligent enough for a child of your age.

46 *Ay:* yes (for abandoning his family and country).

Question

In what tone of voice do you think Lady Macduff is speaking to her son here?

SON
As birds do, mother.

LADY MACDUFF
What, with worms and flies?

SON
With what I get, I mean; and so do they.

LADY MACDUFF
Poor bird! thou 'dst never fear the net, nor lime,
The pit-fall, nor the gin?   35

SON
Why should I, mother?
Poor birds they are not set for.
My father is not dead, for all your saying.

LADY MACDUFF
Yes, he is dead: how wilt thou do for a father?

SON
Nay, how will you do for a husband?   40

LADY MACDUFF
Why, I can buy me twenty at any market.

SON
Then you'll buy 'em to sell again.

LADY MACDUFF
Thou speakest with all thy wit;
And yet, i' faith, with wit enough for thee.

SON
Was my father a traitor, mother?   45

LADY MACDUFF
Ay, that he was.

48 *swears and lies:* makes a vow (of loyalty or of marriage) and then breaks it.
49 *be all . . . so:* are all the people who behave in this way traitors?
57 *enow:* enough.
59 *monkey:* a term of affection, implying that he is mischievous.
    how: what.

Question
What impression have you formed of the young boy?

SON

What is a traitor?

LADY MACDUFF

Why, one that swears and lies.

SON

And be all traitors that do so?

LADY MACDUFF

Every one that does so is a traitor, and must be 50
hanged.

SON

And must they all be hanged that swear and lie?

LADY MACDUFF

Every one.

SON

Who must hang them?

LADY MACDUFF

Why, the honest men.   55

SON

Then the liars and swearers are fools; for there are
liars and swearers enow to beat the honest men, and
hang up them.

LADY MACDUFF

Now God help thee, poor monkey! But how wilt
thou do for a father?   60

SON

If he were dead, you 'ld weep for him: if you would
not, it were a good sign that I should quickly have a
new father.

165

64 *prattler:* chatterbox.
66 *Though in . . . perfect:* but I am well aware of your noble rank.
67 *doubt:* fear.
    nearly: closely.
68 *homely:* humble.
70 *To fright you thus:* to alarm you like this.
    savage: cruel.
71 *To do . . . fell cruelty:* not to warn you (which would be worse) would be ruthless cruelty.
72 *Which . . . person:* which is already too nearly upon you.
76 *laudable:* praiseworthy.
    sometime: sometimes.
81 *unsanctified:* hellish.
82 *such as thou:* fiends like you.

Questions

1 What is the dramatic effect of the Messenger's speech?
2 Which lines spoken by Lady Macduff highlight the way in which the normal moral and religious order has now been reversed in Scotland?

LADY MACDUFF
Poor prattler, how thou talk'st!

Enter a MESSENGER.

MESSENGER
Bless you, fair dame! I am not to you known,   65
Though in your state of honour I am perfect.
I doubt, some danger does approach you nearly:
If you will take a homely man's advice,
Be not found here; hence, with your little ones.
To fright you thus, methinks, I am too savage;   70
To do worse to you were fell cruelty,
Which is too nigh your person. Heaven preserve
        you!
I dare abide no longer.

                                                    Exit

LADY MACDUFF
                        Whither should I fly?
I have done no harm. But I remember now
I am in this earthly world, where to do harm   75
Is often laudable, to do good sometime
Accounted dangerous folly: why then, alas,
Do I put up that womanly defence,
To say, I have done no harm? What are these
        faces?

Enter MURDERERS.

MURDERER
Where is your husband?   80

LADY MACDUFF
I hope, in no place so unsanctified,
Where such as thou may'st find him.

83 *shag-haired:* with shaggy hair.
    egg: unhatched weakling.
84 *fry:* spawn.

Question

Do you find this murder more or less disturbing than the murders of Duncan and Banquo?

---

2 *rather:* instead.
3 *mortal:* deadly.
    good: brave.
4 *Bestride:* defend, like a warrior protecting a fallen companion.
    birthdom: native land.
6 *Strike . : . resounds:* hit heaven so hard that a cry reverberates from the sky.

MURDERER

      He's a traitor.

SON

 Thou liest, thou shag-haired villain!

MURDERER

      What, you egg!

Stabbing him.

 Young fry of treachery!

SON

     He has killed me, mother:
 Run away, I pray you!   85

             Dies

Exit LADY MACDUFF, *crying "Murder!" and pursued by the*
             MURDERERS.

Scene three

England. A room in the King's palace.

Enter MALCOLM *and* MACDUFF.

MALCOLM

 Let us seek out some desolate shade, and there
 Weep our sad bosoms empty.

MACDUFF

      Let us rather
 Hold fast the mortal sword, and like good men
 Bestride our down-fall birthdom. Each new morn,
 New widows howl, new orphans cry; new sorrows 5
 Strike heaven on the face, that it resounds

7 *felt:* suffered.

8 *Like . . . dolour:* similar cries of grief.

8–9 *What . . . believe:* I will only weep for what I believe is true; I will only believe something is true if I know it for a fact.

9 *redress:* put right, avenge.

10 *As:* when.
to friend: favourable.

11 *perchance:* perhaps.

12 *whose sole name:* the mere mention of whose name.

13 *you have loved him well:* you have served him loyally.

14–15 *I am . . . through me:* I am only young, but you may win favour with him by deceiving me.

15 *and wisdom:* and it might be wise.

19–20 *may recoil . . . charge:* is likely to give way under pressure from a king.

21 *That which . . . transpose:* my thoughts cannot change your nature.

22 *Angels . . . fell:* there are still good angels, even though Lucifer – the brightest of all – fell from grace (i.e., his brightness was deceptive).

23–4 *Though all . . . look so:* even if all evil things wore the shining appearance of goodness, good itself would still have a shining appearance too (i.e., it does not follow that appearances are always deceptive).

24 *hopes:* of encouraging Malcolm to act.

25 *Perchance . . . doubts:* perhaps by that action of yours (coming to England) which has made me suspicious.

26 *rawness:* unprotected position.

Questions

1 What doubts is Malcolm expressing about Macduff in this conversation?

2 Explain the dramatic irony of line 14 ('He hath . . . yet').

As if it felt with Scotland, and yelled out
Like syllable of dolour.

MALCOLM

                    What I believe, I'll wail;
What know, believe; and what I can redress,
As I shall find the time to friend, I will   10
What you have spoke, it may be so, perchance.
This tyrant, whose sole name blisters our tongues,
Was once thought honest: you have loved him well;
He hath not touched you yet. I am young; but
    something
You may deserve of him through me, and wisdom 15
To offer up a weak, poor, innocent lamb,
T' appease an angry god.

MACDUFF

I am not treacherous.

MALCOLM

                  But Macbeth is.
A good and virtuous nature may recoil
In an imperial charge. But I shall crave your
    pardon: 20
That which you are, my thoughts cannot transpose:
Angels are bright still, though the brightest fell:
Though all things foul would wear the brows of
    grace,
Yet grace must still look so.

MACDUFF

                  I have lost my hopes.

MALCOLM

Perchance even there, where I did find my doubts. 25
Why in that rawness left you wife and child

27   *motives:* reasons for staying.

     knots of love: emotional ties.

29–30 *Let not . . . safeties:* do not let my suspicions dishonour you – they are my way of protecting myself.

30   *rightly just:* truly honourable.

32   *lay . . . sure:* lay your foundations securely.

33   *goodness:* Malcolm's goodness.

     check: curb.

     wear thou thy wrongs: flaunt your crimes.

34   *The title is affeered:* your right to the throne is legally confirmed (with a pun on 'afeared', implying 'through fear').

36   *space:* realm.

37   *to boot:* in addition.

38   *as in . . . you:* in total certainty that you should be feared.

39   *yoke:* yoke of slavery.

41   *withal:* in addition.

42   *uplifted:* raised in battle.

     in my right: in support of my right to the throne.

43   *England:* the King of England.

44   *goodly thousands:* many thousands of soldiers; 'goodly' also reminds us of the moral worth of the English court.

46   *wear:* carry.

47   *have more . . . before:* will have to endure more evils than it has already.

49   *By:* because of.

     What: who?

Question

What images does Malcolm use to suggest the unhealthiness of Scotland?

(Those precious motives, those strong knots of love)
Without leave-taking? – I pray you,
Let not my jealousies be your dishonours,
But mine own safeties: you may be rightly just,   30
Whatever I shall think.

MACDUFF

               Bleed, bleed, poor country!
Great tyranny, lay thou thy basis sure,
For goodness dare not check thee! wear thou thy
    wrongs;
The title is affeered! – Fare thee well, lord:
I would not be the villain that thou thinkest   35
For the whole space that's in the tyrant's grasp,
And the rich East to boot.

MALCOLM

            Be not offended:
I speak not as in absolute fear of you.
I think our country sinks beneath the yoke;
It weeps, it bleeds; and each new day a gash   40
Is added to her wounds: I think, withal,
There would be hands uplifted in my right;
And here, from gracious England, have I offer
Of goodly thousands: but, for all this,
When I shall tread upon the tyrant's head,   45
Or wear it on my sword, yet my poor country
Shall have more vices than it had before,
More suffer, and more sundry ways than ever,
By him that shall succeed.

MACDUFF

            What should he be?

MALCOLM

It is myself, I mean; in whom I know   50

51 *particulars of vice:* individual vices.
   so grafted: are so implanted.
52 *opened:* come to maturity, as buds open into flowers.
55 *confineless harms:* boundless evils.
57 *top:* surpass.
   grant him: agree that he is.
58 *Luxurious:* lustful.
   avaricious: greedy.
59 *Sudden:* hot-tempered.
   smacking: tasting.
61 *voluptuousness:* wantonness, lust.
   your: Scotland's
63 *cistern:* foul tank.
64 *All ... o'erbear:* would overpower all the barriers of chastity.
65 *will:* lust.
66-7 *Boundless ... tyranny:* immoderate behaviour recognizing no limits is a
   tyranny over the kingdom of a man's nature (usurping reason).
67-8 *hath been ... throne:* caused the premature ending of many prosperous
   reigns.
69 *yet:* despite what you have said.
71 *Convey:* conduct secretly.
   spacious: lavish.
72 *seem cold:* appear chaste.
   time: world.
   hoodwink: deceive.
74 *vulture:* voracious appetite.
75 *as will ... themselves:* as will sacrifice their virtue to the King.
76 *Finding it so inclined:* if the King desires them.

Questions

1 What vice does Malcolm claim would make him a highly unsuitable king?
2 How does Macduff argue against him? How impressive do you find Macduff's argument?

All the particulars of vice so grafted,
That, when they shall be opened, black Macbeth
Will seem as pure as snow; and the poor state
Esteem him as a lamb, being compared
With my confineless harms.

MACDUFF

                Not in the legions   55
Of horrid hell can come a devil more damned
In evils, to top Macbeth.

MALCOLM

             I grant him bloody,
Luxurious, avaricious, false, deceitful,
Sudden, malicious, smacking of every sin
That has a name; but there's no bottom, none,   60
In my voluptuousness: your wives, your daughters,
Your matrons and your maids, could not fill up
The cistern of my lust; and my desire
All continent impediments would o'erbear,
That did oppose my will: better Macbeth   65
Than such an one to reign.

MACDUFF

            Boundless intemperance
In nature is a tyranny; it hath been
Th' untimely emptying of the happy throne,
And fall of many kings. But fear not yet
To take upon you what is yours; you may   70
Convey your pleasures in a spacious plenty,
And yet seem cold – the time you may so hoodwink:
We have willing dames enough; there cannot be
That vulture in you, to devour so many
As will to greatness dedicate themselves.   75
Finding it so inclined.

76 *With this:* in addition.
77 *ill-composed affection:* unbalanced personality.
78 *staunchless:* insatiable.
79 *cut off:* kill.
80 *his:* that man's.
81 *more-having:* gains.
82 *forge:* start, create.
85 *Sticks deeper:* is more ingrained, or cuts like a sword.
   pernicious: wicked, harmful.
86 *summer-seeming:* transitory – heated but brief.
86-7 *it hath been . . . kings:* it has caused the death of all Scotland's murdered
   kings (i.e., they have been killed out of greed).
88 *foisons:* abundant supplies.
   fill up: satisfy.
89 *Of your mere own:* with things that belong to you as royal property.
   these: these vices.
   portable: bearable.
90 *With . . . weighed:* balanced by your virtues.
91 *king-becoming graces:* virtues appropriate to a king.
92 *As:* such as.
   verity: truthfulness.
   stableness: stability.
93 *Bounty:* generosity.
   lowliness: humility.
94 *Devotion:* piety.
95 *relish:* trace.
96 *the division of:* variations on.
   several: separate.
   crime: vice.
98 *concord:* harmony.
99 *Uproar:* throw into confusion.
   confound: destroy.

Questions

1 What qualities, according to Malcolm, are necessary for a ruler?
2 Why is it thematically important to introduce a picture of an ideal
king at this stage in the play?

MALCOLM

                With this, there grows
In my most ill-composed affection such
A staunchless avarice, that, were I king,
I should cut off the nobles for their lands;
Desire his jewels, and this other's house;   80
And my more-having would be as a sauce
To make me hunger more, that I should forge
Quarrels unjust against the good and loyal,
Destroying them for wealth.

MACDUFF

                    This avarice
Sticks deeper, grows with more pernicious root   85
Than summer-seeming lust; and it hath been
The sword of our slain kings: yet do not fear;
Scotland hath foisons to fill up your will,
Of your mere own. All these are portable,
With other graces weighed.   90

MALCOLM

But I have none: the king-becoming graces,
As justice, verity, temperance, stableness,
Bounty, perseverance, mercy, lowliness,
Devotion, patience, courage, fortitude,
I have no relish of them; but abound   95
In the division of each several crime,
Acting it many ways. Nay, had I power, I
    should
Pour the sweet milk of concord into hell,
Uproar the universal peace, confound
All unity on earth.

MACDUFF

           O Scotland! Scotland!   100

104 *untitled:* usurping, with no legal right to the throne.
105 *wholesome:* healthy.
106 *Since that . . . throne:* since the truest heir, Malcolm.
107 *interdiction:* self-accusation.
108 *blaspheme his breed:* slander his parentage.
111 *Died every day she lived:* lived each day as devoutly as if it were to be her last.
112 *repeat'st upon:* recite against.
113 *Hath . . . Scotland:* are the evils, shared by Macbeth, which made me flee from Scotland. Macduff is also implying that he will never be able to return, since Malcolm offers no alternative to Macbeth's wickedness.
115 *Child of:* derived from.
116 *black scruples:* dark doubts.
118 *trains:* plots.
119 *modest:* cautious.
   plucks: holds back.
120 *over-credulous:* too trusting.
   haste: hasty action.
121 *Deal . . . me:* direct the dealings between us.
122 *to:* under.
123 *Unspeak . . . detraction:* withdraw my bad account of myself.
   abjure: renounce.
125 *For strangers:* as foreign.
   yet: still.
126 *Unknown to woman:* a virgin.
   was forsworn: perjured myself.
127 *coveted:* desired.
128 *faith:* promise (of loyalty).

Question

Explain how and why Malcolm has been misleading Macduff. Did his sudden reversal surprise you at all?

MALCOLM

If such a one be fit to govern, speak:
I am as I have spoken.

MACDUFF

                Fit to govern?
No, not to live. – O nation miserable!
With an untitled tyrant, bloody-sceptered!
When shalt thou see thy wholesome days again,   105
Since that the truest issue of thy throne
By his own interdiction stands accused,
And does blaspheme his breed? Thy royal father
Was a most sainted king: the queen that bore thee,
Oft'ner upon her knees than on her feet,   110
Died every day she lived. Fare thee well!
These evils thou repeat'st upon thyself
Hath banished me from Scotland. – O my breast,
Thy hope ends here!

MALCOLM

            Macduff, this noble passion,
Child of integrity, hath from my soul   115
Wiped the black scruples, reconciled my thoughts
To thy good truth and honour. Devilish Macbeth
By many of these trains hath sought to win me
Into his power, and modest wisdom plucks me
From over-credulous haste: but God above   120
Deal between thee and me! for even now
I put myself to thy direction, and
Unspeak mine own detraction; here abjure
The taints and blames I laid upon myself
For strangers to my nature. I am yet   125
Unknown to woman; never was forsworn;
Scarcely have coveted what was mine own;
At no time broke my faith: would not betray

129   *The devil:* even the devil himself.
      delight: take pleasure.
130   *No less ... life:* as much in honesty as in life itself.
133   *here-approach:* coming here.
134   *Old Siward:* the Earl of Northumberland.
135   *at a point:* prepared for battle.
136–7 *the chance ... quarrel:* may the probability of our victory be as certain as the justice of our cause.
142   *stay:* await.
      convinces: defeats.
143   *great assay of art:* best efforts of medical skill.
145   *presently amend:* heal at once.
146   *the evil:* scrofula, known as 'the king's evil'.

Questions

1 How does Macduff react to Malcolm's revelations?
2 Do you think Malcolm has acted fairly in testing him like this?

The devil to his fellow; and delight
No less in truth than life: my first false speaking   130
Was this upon myself. What I am truly
Is thine, and my poor country's, to command:
Whither, indeed, before thy here-approach,
Old Siward, with ten thousand warlike men,
Already at a point, was setting forth.   135
Now we'll together, and the chance of goodness
Be like our warranted quarrel! Why are you silent?

MACDUFF

Such welcome and unwelcome things at once,
'T is hard to reconcile.

Enter a DOCTOR.

MALCOLM

Well, more anon.
(*To the* DOCTOR) Comes the king forth, I pray you? 140

DOCTOR

Ay, sir; there are a crew of wretched souls
That stay his cure: their malady convinces
The great assay of art; but, at his touch,
Such sanctity hath heaven given his hand,
They presently amend.

MALCOLM

I thank you, doctor.   145

Exit DOCTOR

MACDUFF

What's the disease he means?

MALCOLM

'T is called the evil:
A most miraculous work in this good king,

148 *here-remain:* stay.
149 *solicits heaven:* calls on heaven's aid.
150 *strangely-visited:* with unusual or unnatural diseases.
152 *mere:* utter.
153 *golden stamp:* a special gold coin, stamped with the figure of St Michael.
154 *spoken:* said.
155 *succeeding royalty:* his royal descendants.
156 *healing benediction:* blessed gift of healing.
     With: in addition to.
     virtue: power.
159 *speak him:* declare him to be.
161 *gentle:* noble.
     cousin: kinsman.
162 *betimes:* quickly.
163 *means:* circumstances.
165 *know:* recognize.
166–7 *where nothing . . . smile:* where no one, unless he is completely ignorant of the situation, is ever seen to smile.

Question

Edward the Confessor is described as a healer of the sick. Explain the way that imagery of diseases has functioned in the play so far.

Which often, since my here-remain in England,
I have seen him do. How he solicits heaven,
Himself best knows; but strangely-visited people,   150
All swoln and ulcerous, pitiful to the eye,
The mere despair of surgery, he cures;
Hanging a golden stamp about their necks,
Put on with holy prayers: and 't is spoken,
To the succeeding royalty he leaves   155
The healing benediction. With this strange virtue
He hath a heavenly gift of prophecy;
And sundry blessings hang about his throne
That speak him full of grace.

Enter ROSSE.

MACDUFF

                  See, who comes here.

MALCOLM

My countryman; but yet I know him not.   160

MACDUFF

My ever-gentle cousin, welcome hither.

MALCOLM

I know him now. Good God betimes remove
The means that makes us strangers!

ROSSE

                    Sir, amen.

MACDUFF

Stands Scotland where it did?

ROSSE

                Alas, poor country!
Almost afraid to know itself. It cannot   165
Be called our mother, but our grave; where nothing,

169   *marked:* noticed.

170   *modern ecstasy:* commonplace fit of excitement.

170–1   *the dead . . . who:* hardly anyone troubles to ask for whom a funeral bell is ringing.

172   *before the flowers:* before the flowers wither.

173   *Dying . . . sicken:* murdered before they have time to fall ill and die naturally.

173–4   *relation/Too nice:* account that is only too accurate.

175   *That . . . speaker:* news that is only an hour old makes the speaker's audience hiss, because the news is already out of date and has been superseded by new horrors.

176   *teems:* gives birth to, spawns.

Question

Why do you think Rosse tells Macduff that his wife and children are 'well' (line 177) and 'at peace' (line 179)?

But who knows nothing, is once seen to smile;
Where sighs, and groans, and shrieks that rend the
    air
Are made, not marked; where violent sorrow
    seems
A modern ecstasy: the dead man's knell   170
Is there scarce asked for who; and good men's lives
Expire before the flowers in their caps,
Dying or ere they sicken.

MACDUFF

                 O relation
Too nice and yet too true!

MALCOLM

                  What's the newest grief?

ROSSE

That of an hour's age doth hiss the speaker;   175
Each minute teems a new one.

MACDUFF

                  How does my wife?

ROSSE

Why, well.

MACDUFF

       And all my children?

ROSSE

               Well, too.

MACDUFF

The tyrant has not battered at their peace?

ROSSE

No; they were well at peace when I did leave 'em.

180   *Be not a niggard of:* do not hold back in. A 'niggard' is a miser.
181   *tidings:* news (of the murder of Macduff's family).
182   *heavily borne:* sadly carried.
      ran: was circulating.
183   *out:* in the battlefield, against Macbeth.
184   *Which . . . rather:* my belief in which was confirmed.
185   *For that:* because.
      power afoot: army on the march.
186   *of:* for.
      Your eye: Malcolm's presence.
187   *make our women:* make even our women.
188   *doff:* throw off (like clothes).
      Be 't their comfort: let them take comfort.
189   *England:* the King of England.
191–2 *An older . . . out:* there is no more experienced or skilful soldier in all
      of Christendom.
192   *Would:* I wish.
193   *with the like:* with other good news.
194   *would:* should.
195   *latch:* catch.
196   *The general cause:* public matters.
196–7 *a fee-grief ... breast:* private sorrow, belonging to one individual.
199   *Pertains to:* concerns.

Question

What admirable qualities are shown in Malcolm's speech on this page?

MACDUFF

Be not a niggard of your speech: how goes 't?   180

ROSSE

When I came hither to transport the tidings,
Which I have heavily borne, there ran a rumour
Of many worthy fellows that were out;
Which was, to my belief, witnessed the rather,
For that I saw the tyrant's power afoot.   185
Now is the time of help. Your eye in Scotland
Would create soldiers, make our women fight
To doff their dire distresses.

MALCOLM

                    Be 't their comfort,
We are coming thither. Gracious England hath
Lent us good Siward, and ten thousand men;   190
An older and a better soldier none
That Christendom gives out.

ROSSE

                    Would I could answer
This comfort with the like! But I have words
That would be howled out in the desert air,
Where hearing should not latch them.

MACDUFF

                    What concern they?   195
The general cause? or is it a fee-grief
Due to some single breast?

ROSSE

                    No mind that's honest
But in it shares some woe, though the main
    part
Pertains to you alone.

202 *possess them with:* give them, make them hear.
  heaviest sound: saddest words.
204 *surprised:* taken by surprise.
205-7 *to relate . . . you:* to tell you how they died would add your own death (through grief) to what is a whole heap of slaughtered deer. These words include an agonized pun on the word 'dear'.
208 *ne'er . . . brows:* do not hide your face.
210 *Whispers:* whispers to.
  o'er-fraught: over-burdened.
212 *And I . . . thence:* and I had to be away from home at the time!

Question

How does Shakespeare make Macduff's reaction to the news of the massacre both dramatic and moving?

MACDUFF

               If it be mine,
Keep it not from me; quickly let me have it.   200

ROSSE

Let not your ears despise my tongue for ever,
Which shall possess them with the heaviest sound
That ever yet they heard.

MACDUFF

                  Humph! I guess at it.

ROSSE

Your castle is surprised; your wife and babes
Savagely slaughtered: to relate the manner   205
Were, on the quarry of these murdered deer,
To add the death of you.

MALCOLM

                Merciful heaven! –
What, man! ne'er pull your hat upon your brows:
Give sorrow words; the grief that does not speak
Whispers the o'er-fraught heart, and bids it
    break.   210

MACDUFF

My children too?

ROSSE

             Wife, children, servants, all
That could be found.

MACDUFF

             And I must be from thence!
My wife killed too?

ROSSE

           I have said.

214 *Let's make . . . revenge:* let us turn our desire for revenge into a way of alleviating our pain.
216 *He:* probably Malcolm (although possibly Macbeth).
217 *hell-kite:* hellish bird of prey.
218 *dam:* mother.
219 *fell:* cruel.
   Dispute it: stand up to it.
221 *I cannot but remember:* I cannot help remembering.
224 *struck for thee:* killed on my account.
   Naught that I am: worthless creature that I am.
225 *demerits:* sins.
226 *Fell . . . souls:* were their souls slaughtered.
227 *whetstone:* grindstone.
228 *blunt:* numb.
229 *play . . . eyes:* weep.
231 *intermission:* delay (before he faces Macbeth).
   front to front: face to face.
233–4 *if he 'scape . . . too:* if I let him escape, let my punishment be that God forgives him.

Questions

1 Why does Macduff blame himself for the deaths of his wife and children?
2 What resolution does he make at lines 231–3 ('front . . . set him')?

MALCOLM
                              Be comforted:
  Let's make us medicines of our great revenge,
  To cure this deadly grief.   215

MACDUFF
  He has no children. – All my pretty ones?
  Did you say all? – O hell-kite! – All?
  What, all my pretty chickens, and their dam,
  At one fell swoop?

MALCOLM
                      Dispute it like a man.

MACDUFF
                                    I shall do so;
  But I must also feel it as a man: 220
  I cannot but remember such things were,
  That were most precious to me. – Did heaven
      look on,
  And would not take their part? Sinful Macduff!
  They were all struck for thee. Naught that I am,
  Not for their own demerits, but for mine   225
  Fell slaughter on their souls: heaven rest them now!

MALCOLM
  Be this the whetstone of your sword: let grief
  Convert to anger; blunt not the heart, enrage it.

MACDUFF
  O! I could play the woman with mine eyes,
  And braggart with my tongue, – But, gentle heavens, 230
  Cut short all intermission; front to front
  Bring thou this fiend of Scotland and myself;
  Within my sword's length set him; if he 'scape,
  Heaven forgive him too!

234 *This . . . manly:* this is a manly way to speak.
235 *power:* army.
236 *Our lack . . . leave:* we need only to take our leave.
237 *ripe:* ready (like a fruit tree).
     powers above: angels that ward off evil.
238 *Put on their instruments:* arm themselves, or incite their agents on earth.
     cheer: comfort.
239 *The night . . . day:* all times of darkness must come to an end.

Questions

1 Macbeth himself has been present only in the first scene of this Act.
  What is the dramatic effect of this?
2 What impression have you formed of Malcolm from his words and
  actions in Act 4?

MALCOLM

               This time goes manly,
Come, go we to the King: our power is ready;   235
Our lack is nothing but our leave. Macbeth
Is ripe for shaking, and the powers above
Put on their instruments. Receive what cheer you
   may;
The night is long that never finds the day.

Exeunt

1 *watched:* remained awake.
4 *field:* battlefield (to subdue the Scottish rebels).
5 *night-gown:* dressing-gown.
6 *closet:* cabinet for private papers.
9 *perturbation:* disturbance.
  at once: at the same time.
10 *do . . . watching:* behave as though she were awake.
11 *slumbery agitation:* activity while asleep.
12 *actual performances:* specific actions.
14 *after her:* in her words.
15 *meet:* proper.
16 *having no witness:* without a witness to back up her claims the Gentlewoman might be accused of slander.

Questions

1 Why do you think Lady Macbeth is sleep-walking?
2 What do you think Lady Macbeth might be doing with the 'paper' (line 6)?
3 How does the Doctor's way of expressing himself differ from the Gentlewoman's?

Act Five

Scene one

Dunsinane. A room in the castle.

Enter a DOCTOR OF PHYSIC *and a* WAITING-GENTLEWOMAN.

DOCTOR

I have two nights watched with you, but can perceive no truth in your report. When was it she last walked?

GENTLEWOMAN

Since his majesty went into the field, I have seen her rise from her bed, throw her night-gown upon her, 5 unlock her closet, take forth paper, fold it, write upon 't, read it, afterwards seal it, and again return to bed; yet all this while in a most fast sleep.

DOCTOR

A great perturbation in nature, to receive at once the benefit of sleep, and do the effects of watching! 10 In this slumbery agitation, besides her walking and other actual performances, what, at any time, have you heard her say?

GENTLEWOMAN

That, Sir, which I will not report after her.

DOCTOR

You may to me; and 't is most meet you should. 15

GENTLEWOMAN

Neither to you, nor any one, having no witness to confirm my speech.

	taper: candle.
18	*This . . . guise:* there is precisely how she was before.
19	*close:* hidden.
20	*came she by:* did she get.
24	*sense:* powers of sight.
30	*Yet:* even now (after so much washing).
	spot: blood-stain.
31–2	*set down what comes from her:* write down what she says.
32	*satisfy:* confirm.
33	*One; two:* Lady Macbeth imagines she hears a clock, chiming the hour for Duncan's murder.
34	*murky:* dark.
35	*afeard:* afraid.
36–7	*none . . . account:* we will be too powerful to be asked to explain our actions.

Questions

1 What is ironic about the Gentlewoman's comment at lines 21–2 ('she has . . . command')?

2 What is the significance of Lady Macbeth's constant washing of her hands?

Enter LADY MACBETH, *with a taper.*

Lo you! here she comes. This is her very guise, and,
upon my life, fast asleep. Observe her: stand close.

DOCTOR

How came she by that light?   20

GENTLEWOMAN

Why, it stood by her: she has light by her continu-
ally; 't is her command.

DOCTOR

You see, her eyes are open.

GENTLEWOMAN

Ay, but their sense are shut.

DOCTOR

What is it she does now? Look, how she rubs her   25
hands.

GENTLEWOMAN

It is an accustomed action with her, to seem thus
washing her hands. I have known her continue in
this a quarter of an hour.

LADY MACBETH

Yet here's a spot.   30

DOCTOR

Hark! she speaks. I will set down what comes from
her, to satisfy my remembrance the more strongly.

LADY MACBETH

Out, damned spot! out, I say! – One; two; why,
then 't is time to do 't. – Hell is murky. – Fie, my
Lord, fie! a soldier, and afeard? – What need we fear   35
who knows it, when none can call our power to

39 *mark:* note.
42 *mar all:* ruin everything.
43 *starting:* jumpiness.
44 *Go to:* yes indeed.
50 *sorely charged:* painfully burdened.
52 *dignity:* worth.
55 *practice:* medical skill.

Questions

1 Which lines show the listeners that Lady Macbeth was involved in the deaths of Duncan and Lady Macduff?

2 What does the language of Lady Macbeth's speeches reveal about her state of mind?

3 Why is it ironic that the imagery of lines 47–8 ('all ... hand') should be so feminine?

account? – Yet who would have thought the old
man to have had so much blood in him?

DOCTOR

Do you mark that?

LADY MACBETH

The Thane of Fife had a wife: where is she now? –   40
What, will these hands ne'er be clean? – No more o'
that, my lord, no more o' that: you mar all with this
starting.

DOCTOR

Go to, go to: you have known what you should not.

GENTLEWOMAN

She has spoke what she should not, I am sure of   45
that: heaven knows what she has known.

LADY MACBETH

Here's the smell of the blood still: all the perfumes
of Arabia will not sweeten this little hand. Oh! oh!
oh!

DOCTOR

What a sigh is there! The heart is sorely charged.   50

GENTLEWOMAN

I would not have such a heart in my bosom for the
dignity of the whole body.

DOCTOR

Well, well, well –

GENTLEWOMAN

Pray God it be, sir.

DOCTOR

This disease is beyond my practice: yet I have   55

60 *on's:* of his.
61 *Even so:* this too?
67 *Foul ... abroad:* rumours of evil deeds are rife.
68 *infected:* diseased (with guilt).
69 *discharge:* release, tell.
70 *More ... physician:* she has more need of a priest than a doctor.
72 *means of all annoyance:* all means of harming herself.
73 *still:* always.
74 *mated:* stupefied.

Questions

1 At lines 63–4 Lady Macbeth says, 'What's done cannot be undone'.
What earlier lines in the play does this echo?
2 Do you feel sympathy for Lady Macbeth in this scene?

known those which have walked in their sleep, who
have died holily in their beds.

LADY MACBETH
Wash your hands, put on your night-gown; look not
so pale. – I tell you yet again, Banquo's buried: he
cannot come out on's grave.   60

DOCTOR
Even so?

LADY MACBETH
To bed, to bed: there's knocking at the gate. Come,
come, come, come, give me your hand. What's done
cannot be undone. To bed, to bed, to bed.

Exit

DOCTOR
Will she go now to bed?   65

GENTLEWOMAN
Directly.

DOCTOR
Foul whisp'rings are abroad. Unnatural deeds
Do breed unnatural troubles: infected minds
To their deaf pillows will discharge their secrets.
More needs she the divine than the physician. –   70
God, God forgive us all! Look after her;
Remove from her the means of all annoyance.
And still keep eyes upon her. – So, good-night:
My mind she has mated, and amazed my sight.
I think, but dare not speak.   75

GENTLEWOMAN
                          Good-night, good doctor.

Exeunt

201

1 *power:* army.
2 *uncle:* the historical Siward was actually Malcolm's grandfather and Duncan's father-in-law.
3 *dear causes:* strongly felt grievances (i.e., causes of revenge).
4 *bleeding:* bloody.
   alarm: call to arms.
5 *Excite ... man:* arouse even a dead man.
6 *well:* probably.
8 *file:* list.
9 *gentry:* nobles.
10 *unrough:* smooth-skinned, beardless.
11 *Protest ... manhood:* demonstrate for the first time that they are grown men.
15–16 *He cannot ... rule:* he cannot keep his diseased mind (or country) under control.

Question

What is the effect of Macbeth's being referred to only as 'the tyrant' (line 11)?

Scene two

The country near Dunsinane.

Enter, with drums and colours, MENTETH, CATHNESS, ANGUS, LENOX, *and* SOLDIERS.

MENTETH
The English power is near, led on by Malcolm,
His uncle Siward, and the good Macduff.
Revenges burn in them; for their dear causes
Would, to the bleeding and the grim alarm,
Excite the mortified man.

ANGUS
                          Near Birnam wood   5
Shall we well meet them: that way are they coming.

CATHNESS
Who knows if Donalbain be with his brother?

LENOX
For certain, Sir, he is not. I have a file
Of all the gentry: there is Siward's son,
And many unrough youths, that even now   10
Protest their first of manhood.

MENTETH
                          What does the tyrant?

CATHNESS
Great Dunsinane he strongly fortifies.
Some say he's mad: others, that lesser hate him,
Do call it valiant fury; but, for certain,
He cannot buckle his distempered cause   15
With the belt of rule.

ANGUS
                          Now does he feel

17   *sticking:* clinging like gore.
18   *Now ... faith-breach:* every moment now desertions from his ranks remind him of his own breach of faith (to Duncan).
19–20   *only ... love:* only because they are ordered to, not out of personal affection.
23–5   *His ... there:* his frayed nerves for jumping and acting erratically, when all aspects of his nature are in revolt against him.
27   *medicine:* healer, Malcolm.
     sickly weal: sick country.
28–9   *pour we ... us:* sacrifice every drop of blood to cleanse our country. The image also suggests the practice of blood-letting, whereby doctors would lance a vein in the belief that this released the body's impurities.
30   *dew:* water.
     sovereign: royal.

Question

Show how four of the play's main image chains – blood, disease, natural growth and clothes – are used in this exchange to bring together many of the most important themes in *Macbeth*.

---

1   *let them fly all:* let all my thanes desert me.

His secret murders sticking on his hands;
Now minutely revolts upbraid his faith-breach:
Those he commands move only in command,
Nothing in love: now does he feel his title   20
Hang loose about him, like a giant's robe
Upon a dwarfish thief.

MENTETH

                    Who then shall blame
His pestered senses to recoil and start,
When all that is within him does condemn
Itself for being there?

CATHNESS

                    Well; march we on,   25
To give obedience where 't is truly owed:
Meet we the medicine of the sickly weal;
And with him pour we, in our country's purge,
Each drop of us.

LENOX

                    Or so much as it needs
To dew the sovereign flower and drown the weeds. 30
Make we our march towards Birnam.

                                        Exeunt, marching

Scene three

Dunsinane, a room in the castle.

Enter MACBETH, DOCTOR *and* ATTENDANTS.

MACBETH

Bring me no more reports: let them fly all:
Till Birnam wood remove to Dunsinane

205

3 *taint with:* be weakened by.
4 *spirits:* the powers that spoke through the Apparitions.
5 *All mortal consequences:* the outcome of all human affairs.
8 *epicures:* self-indulgent weaklings.
9 *sway by:* control myself with.
10 *sag:* droop.
11 *loon:* fool.
12 *goose look:* the frightened servant is either staring like a goose or has a face like goose-flesh.
14 *over-red thy fear:* cover your paleness with blood.
15 *lily-livered:* cowardly. The liver was thought to be the seat of courage.
    patch: clown.
16 *Death of thy soul:* may you be damned!
    linen: white.
17 *Are counsellors to fear:* persuade others to be afraid.
    whey: the thin liquid remaining when milk has curdled – very pale in colour.
20 *Seyton:* Macbeth's armour-bearer. How do you think this name should be pronounced?
    push: crisis.

Question

What is Macbeth's mood as this scene opens?

I cannot taint with fear. What's the boy Malcolm?
Was he not born of woman? The spirits that know
All mortal consequences have pronounced me thus: 5
"Fear not, Macbeth; no man that's born of woman
Shall e'er have power upon thee." – Then fly, false
     thanes,
And mingle with the English epicures:
The mind I sway by, and the heart I bear,
Shall never sag with doubt, nor shake with fear.   10

Enter a SERVANT.

The devil damn thee black, thou cream-faced
     loon!
Where gott'st thou that goose look?

SERVANT
There is ten thousand –

MACBETH
                    Geese, villain?

SERVANT
                              Soldiers, sir.

MACBETH
Go, prick thy face, and over-red thy fear,
Thou lily-livered boy. What soldiers, patch?   15
Death of thy soul! those linen cheeks of thine
Are counsellors to fear. What soldiers, whey-face?

SERVANT
The English force, so please you.

MACBETH
Take thy face hence. (*Exit* SERVANT) – Seyton! – I
     am sick at heart,
When I behold – Seyton, I say! – This push   20

207

21 *cheer:* hearten, but perhaps also containing the meaning of 'chair' (enthrone).
   disseat: dethrone.
22 *my way of life:* the course of my life.
23 *sere:* dry, withered state.
25 *As:* such as.
26 *in their stead:* in place of them.
27 *mouth-honour:* lip-service.
   breath: mere air.
28 *fain deny:* rather do without.
35 *skirr:* scour, search.

Questions

1 How will Macbeth's old age differ from Duncan's?
2 Traditionally, a tragic hero arouses both our pity and our terror. How far do you think this is true of Macbeth?

Will cheer me ever, or disseat me now.
I have lived long enough: my way of life
Is fall'n into the sere, the yellow leaf;
And that which should accompany old age,
As honour, love, obedience, troops of friends,   25
I must not look to have; but, in their stead,
Curses, not loud but deep, mouth-honour, breath,
Which the poor heart would fain deny, and dare
    not.
Seyton!

Enter SEYTON.

SEYTON

What's your gracious pleasure?

MACBETH

                       What news more?   30

SEYTON

All is confirmed, my lord, which was reported.

MACBETH

I'll fight, till from my bones my flesh be hacked.
Give me my armour.

SEYTON

             'T is not needed yet.

MACBETH

I'll put it on.
Send out more horses, skirr the country round;   35
Hang those that talk of fear. Give me mine
    armour. –
(*To the* DOCTOR) How does your patient, doctor?

DOCTOR

                 Not so sick, my lord,

38 *thick-coming:* crowding upon each other.
    fancies: imaginings.
42 *Raze . . . brain:* erase the troubles imprinted on the mind.
43 *oblivious:* causing forgetfulness.
44 *stuffed:* burdened with guilt.
    perilous stuff: dangerous substance – the melancholy that could cause madness.
45 *weighs upon:* oppresses.
47 *physic:* medicine.
    I'll none of it: I'll have nothing to do with it.
48 *staff:* commander's baton.
50 *Sir:* addressing Seyton.
    despatch: hurry up.
50–1 *cast . . . land:* find the cause of my country's illness by analyzing a urine sample.
51 *her:* Scotland's.
52 *pristine:* first, unsullied.
54 *Pull't off:* remove the armour.
55 *senna:* a plant. Rhubarb and senna were thought to have laxative properties.

Question

Why do you think the Doctor replies that the patient should 'minister to *himself*' (line 46)?

As she is troubled with thick-coming fancies,
That keep her from her rest.

MACBETH
                    Cure her of that:
Canst thou not minister to a mind diseased,   40
Pluck from the memory a rooted sorrow,
Raze out the written troubles of the brain,
And with some sweet, oblivious antidote
Cleanse the stuffed bosom of that perilous
    stuff
Which weighs upon the heart?

DOCTOR
                        Therein the patient   45
Must minister to himself.

MACBETH
Throw physic to the dogs; I'll none of it. –
(*To* SEYTON) Come, put mine armour on; give me
    my staff. –
Seyton, send out. – (*To the* DOCTOR) Doctor, the
    thanes fly from me. –
(*To* SEYTON) Come, Sir, despatch. – (*To the* DOCTOR)
    If thou couldst, doctor, cast   50
The water of my land, find her disease,
And purge it to a sound and pristine health,
I would applaud thee to the very echo,
That should applaud again. – (*To* SEYTON) Pull't off,
    I say. –
(*To the* DOCTOR) What rhubarb, senna, or what
    purgative drug,   55
Would scour these English hence? – Hear'st
    thou of them?

211

58 *it:* the armour.
59 *bane:* destruction.
61 *clear:* safe and untainted by evil.
62 *Profit . . . here:* I would not return here, even for money.

Question

What do Macbeth's various conflicting instructions about his armour reveal about his state of mind?

---

2 *chambers will be safe:* when people can sleep safely in their beds (without being murdered, as Duncan was).
nothing: not at all.

DOCTOR

Ay, my good lord: your royal preparation.
Makes us hear something.

MACBETH

    (To SEYTON) Bring it after me. –
I will not be afraid of death and bane
Till Birnam forest come to Dunsinane.   60

              Exit

DOCTOR

(*Aside*) Were I from Dunsinane away and clear,
Profit again should hardly draw me here.

             Exeunt

Scene four

Country near Dunsinane. A wood in view.

Enter, with drum and colours, MALCOLM, *old* SIWARD *and his* SON, MACDUFF, MENTETH, CATHNESS, ANGUS, LENOX, ROSSE, *and* SOLDIERS, *marching.*

MALCOLM

Cousins, I hope the days are near at hand,
That chambers will be safe.

MENTETH

      We doubt it nothing.

SIWARD

What wood is this before us?

MENTETH

      The wood of Birnam.

4   *hew him:* cut for himself.
5   *bear 't:* carry it.
    shadow: conceal.
6–7 *make . . . us:* ensure that scouts give the wrong information.
8   *no other but:* no other news than that.
9   *Keeps:* remains.
9–10 *will endure . . . before 't:* will allow us to lay siege to it.
11 *advantage:* opportunity.
    to be gone: to escape.
12 *more and less:* those of high and low rank.
    given him the revolt: deserted him.
13 *but constrainèd things:* except wretches who are forced to.
14–16 *Let . . . soldiership:* let our conjectures wait until the actual outcome justifies them, and let us confine ourselves to the practical business of fighting.
17 *due:* at the appropriate time.
18 *What . . . owe:* what our strengths and weaknesses are.
19–20 *Thoughts . . . arbitrate:* speculation can suggest uncertain hopes, but the real issue must be settled by fighting.
21 *advance:* proceed with.

Questions

1 How has the prophecy of the Third Apparition now been fulfilled?
2 Why are Macduff and Siward more cautious than Malcolm?

MALCOLM

    Let every soldier hew him down a bough,
    And bear 't before him: thereby shall we shadow   5
    The numbers of our host, and make discovery
    Err in report of us.

SOLDIERS

               It shall be done.

SIWARD

    We learn no other but the confident tyrant
    Keeps still in Dunsinane, and will endure
    Our setting down before 't.

MALCOLM

                  'T is his main hope;   10
    For where there is advantage to be gone,
    Both more and less have given him the revolt,
    And none serve with him but constrainèd things,
    Whose hearts are absent too.

MACDUFF

                Let our just censures
    Attend the true event, and put we on   15
    Industrious soldiership.

SIWARD

             The time approaches
    That will, with due decision, make us know
    What we shall say we have, and what we owe.
    Thoughts speculative their unsure hopes relate,
    But certain issue strokes must arbitrate;   20
    Towards which advance the war.

                          Exeunt, marching

3   *them:* the besiegers.
4   *ague:* fever.
5   *forced:* reinforced.
6   *dareful:* boldly.
    beard to beard: face to face.
7   *home:* decisively.
10 *The time . . . cooled:* there was a time when it would have made me shiver.
11 *night-shriek:* cry in the night.
    fell of hair: scalp with hair on it.
12 *dismal treatise:* sinister tale.
13 *As life were in 't:* as if it were alive.
14 *Direness:* horror.
15 *Cannot once start me:* can never startle me now.
    Wherefore: what was the reason for?

Questions

1   What does Macbeth mean by 'I have supped full with horrors' (line 13)?
2   What is the dramatic effect of the news of Lady Macbeth's death at this point?
3   How do you imagine Lady Macbeth has died?

Scene five

Dunsinane. Within the castle.

Enter, with drum and colours, MACBETH, SEYTON, *and* SOLDIERS.

MACBETH

Hang out our banners on the outward walls;
The cry is still, "They come!" Our castle's strength
Will laugh a siege to scorn; here let them lie,
Till famine and the ague eat them up.
Were they not forced with those that should be ours,   5
We might have met them dareful, beard to beard,
And bear them backward home. (*A cry within, of women*) What is that noise?

SEYTON

It is the cry of women, my good lord.

Exit

MACBETH

I have almost forgot the taste of fears.
The time has been, my senses would have cooled?   10
To hear a night-shriek; and my fell of hair
Would, at a dismal treatise, rouse and stir,
As life were in 't. I have supped full with horrors:
Direness, familiar to my slaughterous thoughts,
Cannot once start me.

Re-enter SEYTON.

Wherefore was that cry?   15

SEYTON

The queen, my lord, is dead.

217

17   *hereafter:* later.
18   *a time for such a word:* a convenient time for such news.
20   *Creeps . . . day:* one day creeps after another in the same trivial way.
21   *To . . . time:* until the very last word in the book of life.
22–3 *all . . . dusty death:* every day of our lives has marked the end of some
      other person's life – like a candle showing him the way upstairs to his
      death-bed.
24   *poor:* pathetic.
      player: actor.
25   *struts and frets his hour:* tries in vain to show dignity and passion in his
      hour on stage.
31   *should:* would.
      say: declare.
34   *anon:* all at once.
38   *grove:* forest.

Questions

1 Why is Macbeth unable to mourn his wife's death?
2 In what tone of voice do you think an actor should speak line 19
  ('Tomorrow . . . tomorrow')?
3 Explain how the imagery of lines 19–28 expresses Macbeth's mood.
  What effect does this speech have on your view of Macbeth?

MACBETH

    She should have died hereafter:
There would have been a time for such a word. –
Tomorrow, and tomorrow, and tomorrow,
Creeps in this petty pace from day to day,   20
To the last syllable of recorded time;
And all our yesterdays have lighted fools
The way to dusty death. Out, out, brief candle!
Life's but a walking shadow, a poor player
That struts and frets his hour upon the stage,   25
And then is heard no more: it is a tale
Told by an idiot, full of sound and fury,
Signifying nothing.

Enter a MESSENGER.

    Thou com'st to use thy tongue; thy story quickly.

MESSENGER   30

    Gracious my lord,
I should report that which I say I saw,
But know not how to do 't.

MACBETH

                Well, say, sir.

MESSENGER

    As I did stand my watch upon the hill,
I looked toward Birnam, and anon, methought,
The wood began to move.

MACBETH

              Liar and slave!   35

MESSENGER

    Let me endure your wrath, if 't be not so.
Within this three mile may you see it coming;
I say, a moving grove.

40 *famine cling thee:* you shrivel up with starvation.
    sooth: true.
41 *thou dost for me as much:* you do the same to me.
42 *pull in resolution:* check my resolute course.
43 *equivocation:* indirect lying, deception.
44 *lies like truth:* deceives by appearing truthful.
46 *Arm:* on with my armour!
    out: out into battle!
47 *avouches:* asserts.
48 *tarrying:* remaining.
49 *the sun:* life.
50 *estate:* order.
51 *wrack:* ruin.
52 *harness:* armour.

Question

Do you find anything to admire in Macbeth's last words in this scene?

---

2 *show like those you are:* reveal yourselves as soldiers.
4 *first battle:* first division of the army, the main force.
5 *upon 's:* upon us.
6 *order:* plan.

MACBETH

                    If thou speak'st false,
Upon the next tree shalt thou hang alive,
Till famine cling thee: if thy speech be sooth,   40
I care not if thou dost for me as much. –
I pull in resolution, and begin
To doubt th' equivocation of the fiend,
That lies like truth: "Fear not, till Birnam wood
Do come to Dunsinane"; – and now a wood   45
Comes toward Dunsinane, – Arm, arm, and out!
If this which he avouches does appear,
There is nor flying hence, nor tarrying here.
I 'gin to be aweary of the sun,
And wish th' estate o' th' world were now undone. 50
Ring the alarum bell! – Blow, wind! come, wrack!
At least we'll die with harness on our back.

                            Exeunt

Scene six

The same. A plain before the castle.

Enter, with drum and colours, MALCOLM, *old* SIWARD,
MACDUFF, *etc., and their army, with boughs.*

MALCOLM

Now, near enough: your leafy screens throw down,
And show like those you are. – (*To old* SIWARD) you,
    worthy uncle,
Shall, with my cousin, your right noble son,
Lead our first battle: worthy Macduff and we
Shall take upon 's what else remains to do,   5
According to our order.

7   *Do we but:* if we only.
    power: troops.
10 *clamorous:* noisy.
    harbingers: forerunners, heralds.

Question

Why do you think Act Five contains so many short scenes? What
effect do they have?

---

1 *tied me to a stake:* trapped me, as a bear is tied to a post to be baited by
   dogs in a 'course' (bout) – see line 2.
2 *What's he:* what sort of man is he?
6 *though thou:* even if.

SIWARD
                    Fare you well. –
Do we but find the tyrant's power tonight,
Let us be beaten, if we cannot fight.

MACDUFF
Make all our trumpets speak; give them all breath,
Those clamorous harbingers of blood and death.   10

Exeunt. Alarms continued

Scene seven

The same. Another part of the plain.

Enter MACBETH.

MACBETH
They have tied me to a stake: I cannot fly,
But, bear-like, I must fight the course. – What's he
That was not born of woman? Such a one
Am I to fear, or none.

Enter YOUNG SIWARD.

YOUNG SIWARD
What is thy name?

MACBETH
                    Thou'lt be afraid to hear it.   5

YOUNG SIWARD
No; though thou call'st thyself a hotter name
Than any is in hell.

MACBETH
                    My name's Macbeth.

10 *abhorrèd:* hated, loathed.
11 *I'll prove the lie:* I'll prove it to be a lie.
15 *with no stroke of mine:* without my being the person to kill you.
16 *still:* forever.
18 *staves:* spear-shafts.
    either thou: either I strike at you (addressing Macbeth).
20 *undeeded:* unused.
    shouldst be: are likely to be.
21 *By . . . clatter:* judging by this racket.
    greatest note: highest eminence or rank.
22 *bruited:* proclaimed by the noise.

Question

Who else had 'Kernes' (line 17) – Irish mercenaries – in his army?
What is the significance of this?

YOUNG SIWARD

The devil himself could not pronounce a title
More hateful to mine ear.

MACBETH

No, nor more fearful.

YOUNG SIWARD

Thou liest, abhorrèd tyrant: with my sword   10
I'll prove the lie thou speak'st.

They fight, and YOUNG SIWARD *is slain.*

MACBETH

Thou wast born of woman: –
But swords I smile at, weapons laugh to scorn,
Brandished by man that's of a woman born.

Exit

Alarms. Enter MACDUFF.

MACDUFF

That way the noise is. – (*Calling to* MACBETH)
Tyrant, show thy face:
If thou be'st slain, and with no stroke of mine,   15
My wife and children's ghosts willl haunt me still.
I cannot strike at wretched Kernes, whose arms
Are hired to bear their staves: either thou,
Macbeth,
Or else my sword, with an unbattered edge,
I sheathe again undeeded. There thou shouldst be;   20
By this great clatter, one of greatest note
Seems bruited. (*Aside*) Let me find him, Fortune!
And more I beg not.

Exit. Alarm

24   *gently rendered:* surrendered peaceably.
27   *The . . . yours:* you have almost won the day.
29   *strike beside us:* fight on our side, or aim their blows to miss us.

1   *play the Roman fool:* traditionally, defeated Roman generals held it honourable to kill themselves after losing a battle, in order to avoid capture.
2   *Whiles I see lives:* as long as I see living enemies.
3   *Do better upon them:* suit them better.
4   *Of all men else:* more than all other men.
5   *charged:* burdened.

Question

Do you think Macbeth refuses to fight Macduff out of fear or remorse?

Enter MALCOLM *and old* SIWARD.

SIWARD

This way, my lord; – the castle's gently rendered:
The tyrant's people on both sides do fight;   25
The noble thanes do bravely in the war.
The day almost itself professes yours,
And little is to do.

MALCOLM

               We have met with foes
That strike beside us.

SIWARD

                  Enter, Sir, the castle.

                       Exeunt. Alarm

Scene eight

Another part of the field.

Enter MACBETH.

MACBETH

Why should I play the Roman fool, and die
On mine own sword? Whiles I see lives, the gashes
Do better upon them.

Enter MACDUFF.

MACDUFF

              Turn, hell-hound, turn!

MACBETH

Of all men else I have avoided thee:
But get thee back, my soul is too much charged   5
With blood of thine already.

8   *Than . . . out:* than words can describe you.
    Thou losest labour: you are wasting your energy.
9   *intrenchant:* uncuttable.
10   *keen:* sharp.
    impress: make an impression on.
11   *vulnerable crests:* the helmets of men you can hurt.
12   *must not yield:* is fated not to surrender.
13   *Despair thy charm:* despair of this charm on your life.
14   *angel:* evil angel.
    still: always.
15–16   *was from . . . ripped:* was born prematurely, by a caesarean operation.
18   *cowed:* depressed.
    better part of man: manly spirit.
19   *juggling:* cheating.
20   *palter:* trifle.
    in . . . sense: with words that can have two different meanings.
21–2   *That . . . hope:* that keep their promises in a literal way, but deceive us in the hopes those promises raise.
24   *gaze o' th' time:* public spectacle.
25   *monsters:* freaks.
26   *Painted . . . underwrit:* advertised by a painting hung from a pole, with this caption underneath.

Question

All of the three prophecies made by the Apparitions have now come true, although not in the way Macbeth imagined. Looking back on that scene, how do you now interpret the images (an armed head, a bloody child, a crowned child with a tree in his hand) that accompanied the prophecies?

MACDUFF

> I have no words;
> My voice is in my sword: thou bloodier villain
> Than terms can give thee out!

They fight.

MACBETH

> Thou losest labour:
> As easy may'st thou the intrenchant air
> With thy keen sword impress, as make me bleed: 10
> Let fall thy blade on vulnerable crests:
> I bear a charmèd life, which must not yield
> To one of woman born.

MACDUFF

> Despair thy charm;
> And let the angel whom thou still hast served
> Tell thee, Macduff was from his mother's womb   15
> Untimely ripped.

MACBETH

> Accursèd be that tongue that tells me so,
> For it hath cowed my better part of man:
> And be these juggling fiends no more believed,
> That palter with us in a double sense,   20
> That keep the word of promise to our ear,
> And break it to our hope. – I'll not fight with
>   thee.

MACDUFF

> Then yield thee, coward,
> And live to be the show and gaze o' th' time:
> We'll have thee, as our rarer monsters are,   25
> Painted upon a pole, and underwrit,
> "Here may you see the tyrant".

229

29 *baited . . . curse:* jeered at, persecuted by the curses of common people.
31 *opposed:* set as my opponent.
32 *try the last:* fight to the end.
33 *lay on:* fight on.
34 *Hold, enough:* stop, no more!

Questions

1 Do you find Macbeth's death heroic?
2 Re-read carefully Act 1, Scene 4, lines 5–11 describing the death of the previous Thane of Cawdor. Do you find Macbeth's death any more or less admirable than that of his predecessor?

---

1 *would:* wish
   we miss: who are missing.
2 *go off:* die
   by these I see: judging from the number of bodies I see around us.
5 *paid . . . debt:* died the death due to a warrior.
7 *The which . . . confirmed:* no sooner had his bravery confirmed that he was a man.
8 *unshrinking . . . fought:* post where he fought without flinching.

MACBETH

                    I will not yield,
To kiss the ground before young Malcolm's feet,
And to be baited with the rabble's curse.
Though Birnam wood be come to Dunsinane,   30
And thou opposed, being of no woman born,
Yet I will try the last: before my body
I throw my warlike shield: lay on, Macduff;
And damned be him that first cries, "Hold,
    enough!"

Exeunt, fighting. Alarms. Re-enter fighting, and MACBETH *is slain.*

Scene nine

Within the castle.

Retreat. Flourish. Enter, with drum and colours, MALCOLM, *old* SIWARD, ROSSE, THANES *and* SOLDIERS.

MALCOLM

    I would the friends we miss were safe arrived.

SIWARD

    Some must go off; and yet, by these I see,
    So great a day as this is cheaply bought.

MALCOLM

    Macduff is missing, and your noble son.

ROSSE

    Your son, my lord, has paid a soldier's debt: 5
    He only lived but till he was a man;
    The which no sooner had his prowess confirmed,
    In the unshrinking station where he fought,
    But like a man he died.

12 *Had ... before:* were his wounds on the front of his body (proving that he was facing the enemy)?

14 *hairs:* hairs on my head, with a sorrowful pun on 'heirs'.

16 *knell is knolled:* funeral bell is tolled.

18 *parted well:* died honourably.
   paid his score: paid his debts nobly (by doing his duty).

20 *stands:* is upheld (on the point of a spear).

21 *the time is free:* the age is set free (from tyranny).

22 *compassed ... pearl:* surrounded by nobles, like pearls encircling a crown.

23 *That ... minds:* who are thinking the words I have greeted you with ('Hail, King!').

Question

Do you find old Siward's attitude to his son's death admirable?

SIWARD

Then he is dead?

ROSSE

Ay, and brought off the field. Your cause of
   sorrow   10
Must not be measured by his worth, for then
It hath no end.

SIWARD

Had he his hurts before?

ROSSE

Ay, on the front.

SIWARD

Why, then, God's soldier be he!
Had I as many sons as I have hairs,
I would not wish them to a fairer death: 15
And so, his knell is knolled.

MALCOLM

He's worth more sorrow,
And that I'll spend for him.

SIWARD

He's worth no more;
They say he parted well, and paid his score:
And so, God be with him! – Here comes newer
   comfort.

Enter MACDUFF *with* MACBETH's *head.*

MACDUFF

Hail, King! for so thou art. Behold, where stands 20
Th' usurper's cursèd head: the time is free.
I see thee compassed with thy kingdom's pearl,
That speak my salutation in their minds;

24 *de.ire aloud:* ask to speak out.
27 *reckon . . . loves:* reward the love of each one of you.
28 *make us even with you:* cancel our debt to you.
30 *In such . . . named:* named with this honourable title.
    What's . . . do: the other things to be done.
31 *Which . . . time:* which should be started afresh with the new era.
32 *As:* such as.
33 *snares:* traps.
    watchful: suspicious.
34 *Producing forth:* bringing out of hiding.
    ministers: agents.
36 *by self and violent hands:* by her own violent hands.
37 *Took off her life:* killed herself.
    what needful else: everything else that needs to be done.
38 *calls upon us:* demands our attention.
    Grace: God.
39 *measure:* due order.

Questions

1 Do you agree with Malcolm that Macbeth and his wife were a
  'dead butcher' and a 'fiend-like queen' (line 35)?
2 Do you consider this a satisfying ending to the play?

Whose voices I desire aloud with mine, –
Hail, King of Scotland!

ALL

                    Hail, King of Scotland!   25

Flourish.

MALCOLM

We shall not spend a large expense of time
Before we reckon with your several loves,
And make us even with you. My thanes and kins-
    men,
Henceforth be earls, the first that ever Scotland
In such an honour named. What's more to do,   30
Which would be planted newly with the time, –
As calling home our exiled friends abroad,
That fled the snares of watchful tyranny;
Producing forth the cruel ministers
Of this dead butcher, and his fiend-like queen,   35
Who, as 't is thought, by self and violent hands
Took off her life; – this, and what needful else
That calls upon us, by the grace of Grace,
We will perform in measure, time and place,
So thanks to all at once, and to each one,   40
Whom we invite to see us crowned at Scone.

Flourish. Exeunt

Studying *Macbeth*

Text and performance

The earliest surviving text of *Macbeth* was printed in 1623 – seven years after Shakespeare's death. We know, however, that the play was actually written very much earlier, during the first six months of 1606. Shakespeare was then forty-two years old – at the very top of his career as a professional playwright and at the very height of his imaginative and creative powers.

Shakespeare's acting company (the King's Men) was the most honoured in the land, for – as its title suggests – the patron was none other than the King himself. King James I had come to the throne in 1603, on the death of Queen Elizabeth I, and Shakespeare had immediately won royal recognition and favour (he had even been awarded the honour of a special livery for the coronation procession). Moreover, it is almost certain that the first ever performance of *Macbeth* – in July or August 1606 – was by royal command. It was staged as a private court performance, most probably at Hampton Court, as part of the celebrations commemorating the visit to England of King Christian IV of Denmark, James's brother-in-law.

It is often suggested that *Macbeth* may have been written with the proposed royal visit specifically in mind (one explanation that is often given for its shortness, for example, is that Shakespeare knew that King James tended to get bored rather quickly, and so kept things deliberately brief!). But we can never now be really sure to what extent (if at all) this was so. One thing *does* seem clear, however: of all Shakespeare's plays, this offers beyond doubt the most direct and personal tribute to his royal patron. *Macbeth* is a play about a king, and for a king.

James I and Macbeth

James I of England was also James VI of Scotland. He was Scottish by birth – born into the royal Stuart family – and his accession to the English throne had united the thrones of England and Scotland. Naturally, therefore, a play about an ancient King of Scotland was of immediate personal interest to him – not least since it included several of his ancestors among its characters.

James had a deep affection for his native country and for its people, and ancient Scotland is evoked with compelling power in *Macbeth*. The play is like a vast canvas that paints for us Scotland's stark landscapes, its castles, woods and hills, its weather and its wildlife; even the place-names – Inverness, Scone, Colme-kill, Fife and Dunsinane – give an atmosphere of strange and haunting beauty. The Scottish character is also depicted fondly. For although the caricature of the Porter may give us a diverting picture of a typically dour, hard-drinking Scot, it is above all the nobility of the Scottish temperament – with its courage, its stoicism, and its fervent patriotism – that so dominates the play.

James's immediate family heritage was also a source of great pride to him. In contrast to the infertility of the English Tudors, for example (Queen Mary I and Queen Elizabeth I had both died childless), the Scottish House of Stuart could boast a dynasty of eight successive monarchs who could be traced back in an unbroken line to the union between Walter Stuart (supposed descendant of Banquo) and a daughter of King Robert the Bruce (descended from Duncan). This royal line is celebrated in *Macbeth* in the pageant of eight kings that materializes in Act 4, Scene 1 – to Macbeth's cries of amazement and horrified disbelief:

Why do you show me this? – a fourth? – Start, eyes!
What! will the line stretch out to th' crack of doom.
Another yet? – A seventh? – I'll see no more:
(Act 4, Scene 1, lines 116–18)

The eighth king in this procession, of course, is James himself, which intensified still further the significance of this episode to a court audience watching spellbound in 1606. And by representing him as carrying a mirror that shows 'many more' future descendants who will also carry the 'two-fold balls and treble sceptres' that signify rule over both England and Scotland, Shakespeare was paying King James the formal compliment of assuring him that the chain of Stuart kings would continue to rule far into the future.

Such an assurance must have been especially welcome to King James in 1606. For 1605 had been the year of the Gunpowder Plot – an attempt by a group of Catholics, angered by discrimination against their religion, to blow up both the King and the Houses of Parliament. The plot had failed, but both England and the King had been badly shaken by the attempt – just as waves of horror and shock are shown to follow the 'dire combustion and confused events' of *Macbeth*.

Macbeth contains several very direct and specific references to the Gunpowder Plot. For example, when Lady Macbeth tells Macbeth to:

> . . . look like the innocent flower
> But be the serpent under 't . . .
>
> (Act 1, Scene 5, lines 65–6)

a contemporary audience would be reminded immediately of the medallion that was struck to commemorate the discovery of the plot, which showed a serpent lurking hidden beneath flowers. Moreover, the Porter's scorn for 'equivocation' (the telling of misleading half-truths) would remind them of the trial in March 1606 of Father Henry Garnet for his part in the plot (see note on page 70). ''Faith,' cries the Porter:

> . . . here's an equivocator that could swear in both the scales against either scale; who committed treason enough for God's

sake, yet could not equivocate to heaven ...

> (Act 2, Scene 3, lines 8–11)

During his trial, Garnet had claimed that his lies on oath had been mere 'equivocation', and were therefore a justifiable defence.

For King James, however, the central and crucial parallel between the events of the Gunpowder Plot and *Macbeth* was much more direct and individual. It was the parallel of *situation*. *Macbeth* shows the consequences of the murder of a king, a subject all too close to James's own heart. And in particular, its moral framework echoes and supports his own deep-rooted belief that a king was God's representative on earth: a crime against a king was therefore also an offence against God.

In *Macbeth*, Duncan is described by Macbeth himself as 'gracious' and by Macduff as 'a most sainted King'; his body was 'The Lord's anointed temple', and his murder was thus shockingly 'sacrilegious'. Similarly, Edward the Confessor, King of England, is associated – even more strongly – with divinity. He is known as the 'holy King' and his court is a haven of healing and prayer:

> ... sundry blessings hang about his throne
> That speak him full of grace.
>
> (Act 4, Scene 3, lines 158–9)

King Edward has special powers from God: a 'heavenly gift of prophecy' and – most significantly for James, who by 1606 had himself begun to 'touch' to cure scrofula (the 'King's Evil') – the ability to heal the sick:

> ... there are a crew of wretched souls
> That stay his cure: their malady convinces
> The great assay of art; but, at his touch,

Such sanctity hath heaven given his hand,
They presently amend.

(Act 4, Scene 3, lines 141–5)

Macbeth focuses very potently on James I's preoccupations as a king. Banquo's 'royalty of nature' is admired even by Macbeth himself:

. . . 't is much he dares;
And, to that dauntless temper of his mind,
He hath a wisdom that does guide his valour
To act in safety.

(Act 3, Scene 1, lines 50–3)

And the whole play celebrates forcefully the 'king-becoming graces' of:

. . . justice, verity, temperance, stableness,
Bounty, perseverance, mercy, lowliness,
Devotion, patience, courage, fortitude

(Act 4, Scene 3, lines 92–4)

Reassuringly, moreover, it also demonstrates that wise, courageous and righteous leadership can restore unity and order to a troubled nation.

But *Macbeth* did not only appeal to·James's interests as a king: it appealed also to his interests as a man. In particular, it focuses colourfully on witchcraft and black magic about which he felt a strong and lasting curiosity. Witches and devils first began to fascinate James when it was discovered that a coven of Scottish witches had cast evil spells to try to disrupt his return voyage from Denmark, after his marriage to Christian IV's sister. Their confessions, published in 1591, made compulsive reading. One of the witches – Agnes Seaton – gave a graphic account of how their magic rites had included collecting toad venom, christening a cat and sailing out to sea in a sieve – taking along with them a dismembered corpse which they cast into the water. Highly intrigued by such lurid details – especially as his ship *had* been delayed by mysterious winds! – James attended the trial with great interest. In 1597 he wrote a treatise on witchcraft called *Demonologie*, which was published in 1603, and in the course of his reign he investigated many strange cases of witchcraft and demonic possession.

No case could ever be so immediately relevant to him as the case which had involved him personally, however. And it was to the details of that case that Shakespeare chose to relate his own 'weird sisters' – with their harassment of ships, their sieve-sailing exploits, their cat 'familiar' and – above all – the disgusting coagulation of severed corpses and toad venom that bubbles so hypnotically in their cauldron:

> Round about the cauldron go;
> In the poisoned entrails throw.
> Toad, that under cold stone
> Days and nights has thirty-one
> Sweltered venom, sleeping got,
> Boil thou first i' th' charmèd pot.

(Act 4, Scene 1, lines 4–9)

The source of Macbeth

A story that could combine a Scottish setting with a history of the Stuart family, a moral treatise on the sanctity of kings *and* a coven of witches was certainly something of an inspired choice as a play to please the King! Shakespeare found it in Holinshed's *Chronicles of England, Scotland and Ireland*, published in 1577. Or – more exactly – he found in Holinshed's work a wealth of historical and legendary material that he could then expand, contract or adapt at will, to suit his own dramatic purposes. Perhaps, indeed, his attention had already been drawn to the possibilities and the aptness of the tale of Macbeth by an entertainment that had greeted James I in August 1605 on his visit to Oxford (an occasion at which Shakespeare himself might even have been present). In celebration of the King's famous descent from Banquo, Dr Matthew Gwinn – a fellow of St John's College – had arranged for the royal guest to be welcomed by three students representing the 'three women in strange and wild apparel' who, according to Holinshed's narrative, had hailed Macbeth and Banquo with their prophecies.

The events of Act 1, Scene 3 of *Macbeth*, which describes the first meeting with the witches on the 'blasted heath' scarred by lightning and battle, are taken very directly from this account in Holinshed's *Chronicles* (the only other episode which is transcribed so faithfully from the original is the 'testing' of Macduff by Malcolm). The name by which the witches are known also comes straight from Holinshed: he called them 'the Weird Sisters, that is (as ye would say) the goddesses of destiny'.

Nevertheless, Shakespeare's witches still differ very significantly from those in the *Chronicles*. Firstly, they are very much Scottish folk-lore witches – 'withered' hags, with 'choppy' fingers, thin lips and bearded chins – rather than the nebulous 'goddesses . . . nymphs or fairies' of Holinshed's account. But, even more importantly, in *Macbeth* they are to reappear, acquiring cumulative force as a powerful symbol of the recurrence and persistence of evil. In Holinshed's story, Macbeth is told to beware of Macduff by 'certain wizards' in whose words he 'put great confidence', and the promises that he will not be killed by a man born of woman nor until Birnam Wood comes to Dunsinane are made by 'a certain witch'. In *Macbeth*, however, these prophecies are all attributed to the Weird Sisters themselves, the evil 'instruments of darkness' whose presence and influence are to become as unavoidable to Macbeth as the wicked thoughts within his own mind and soul.

Many other interesting differences can be traced between

Macbeth and the *Chronicles*. The historical Duncan, for example, was killed by Macbeth in battle. In *Macbeth*, however, Shakespeare opts to heighten intrigue and suspense by weaving a far more elaborate and haunting murder plot; and, in doing so, he introduces details from two other stories recounted in Holinshed's history. One of these is the description of the murder of King Duff by Donwald, captain of the castle of Forres. From this account Shakespeare drew his initial inspiration for the character of Lady Macbeth: Donwald 'abhorred the act greatly in his heart', but was persuaded to commit murder by his cruel and ambitious wife. Moreover, the King Duff story also supplied Shakespeare with a sinister and treacherous murder scheme (Donwald killed Duff – his King and guest – as he slept in his bed, and then slew his drugged servants in order to suggest their guilt), as well as with a dreadful catalogue of the unnatural happenings that were said to follow the death of the King. Compare the following account (from Holinshed) with the horrified discussion between Ross and the Old Man in Act 2, Scene 4 of *Macbeth*:

> For the space of six months together ... there appeared no sun by day, nor moon by night, in any part of the realm, but still was the sky covered with continual clouds, and sometimes such outrageous winds arose with lightnings and tempests, that the people were in great fear of present destruction ... horses in Lothian, being of singular beauty and swiftness, did eat their own flesh ... There was a sparrow-hawk also strangled by an owl.

The other main story that influenced the way in which Duncan's murder is presented in *Macbeth* was Holinshed's account of King Kenneth, who killed his own nephew. After the deed the murderous King was unable to sleep, constantly haunted by a voice that threatened him with vengeance. In *Macbeth*, of course, Shakespeare externalized the idea of haunting in the form of the ghost of Banquo (the historical

Banquo was never sighted as a ghost, and was not even killed until *after* the banquet). But most importantly of all, he took and developed the theme of sleeplessness with a fervent and poetic intensity.

Macbeth – the killer of a sleeping king – comes to see himself as the destroyer of sleep itself, and is racked by near-hysterical terror:

> Methought I heard a voice cry, 'Sleep no more!
> Macbeth does murder sleep'
>
> (Act 2, Scene 2, lines 34–5)

Sleep is the blessing of the innocent:

> ... the innocent sleep;
> Sleep, that knits up the ravelled sleave of care,
> The death of each day's life, sore labour's bath,
> Balm of hurt minds ...
>
> (Act 2, Scene 2, lines 35–8)

And Macbeth and Lady Macbeth, guilty of treason and murder, are fated never to find peace in 'the season of all natures, sleep'; instead, their nights are to be disrupted eternally by:

> ... the affliction of these terrible dreams
> That shake us nightly.
>
> (Act 3, Scene 2, lines 18–19)

Lack of sleep is to destroy Lady Macbeth's frail hold on reality. For Macbeth, it is to serve as a perpetual and ironic reminder of the futility of his crime:

> ... Better be with the dead
> Whom we, to gain our place, have sent to peace,
> Than on the torture of the mind to lie

In restless ecstasy. Duncan is in his grave;
After life's fitful fever he sleeps well;
Treason has done his worst: nor steel, nor poison,
Malice domestic, foreign levy, nothing
Can touch him further.

(Act 3, Scene 2, lines 19–26)

In his handling of the main story line of *Macbeth*, Shakespeare made many changes from Holinshed's *Chronicles*. For example, he narrowed the time scale very significantly – to create a terrifying sense of the speed governing both the spread of evil and the coming of divine retribution. And he also simplified characters and situations, presenting a much starker – more emblematic – conflict of good and evil than was evident in the *Chronicles*. The real Banquo, for instance, was a treacherous character who knew of the plot against Duncan's life. The real Duncan was 'a dull coward and a slothful person', whose naming of his son Malcolm as heir to the throne while still a minor was a violation of Macbeth's own genuine and legal right to the succession. And the real Macbeth – who was initially welcomed as monarch – reigned justly for ten years before murdering Banquo and embarking on a seven-year period of tyrannical rule.

The brilliance with which Shakespeare adapted the routine historical source material of *Macbeth* to shape it into so powerful a study of human evil is the hallmark of a genius – a vital part of his extraordinary poetic and dramatic gift. But perhaps it is worth remembering that not all of his alterations to the historical account were made on purely artistic grounds. According to the *Chronicles*, Macbeth and Banquo did not only defeat the rebel Macdonwald and King Sweno of Norway. They also routed a Danish army, sent by King Canute. And the absence of any reference to this in *Macbeth* probably has far more to do with the presence in the audience of King James's Danish brother-in-law than with the finer points of dramatic theory!

Shakespeare's theatre

Shakespeare was a man of the theatre. Since 1590 the theatre had been his life – as an actor, as an investor, as a manager and as a playwright. And images drawn from the world of the theatre are at the very heart of *Macbeth*, making it in many senses an intensely personal play. Macbeth's response to the realisation that the witches' second prophecy has been fulfilled is expressed in the language of the stage:

> Two truths are told
> As happy prologues to the swelling act
> Of the imperial theme.
>
> (Act 1, Scene 3, lines 127–9)

So, too, his mood of weary despair towards the end of his life is given theatrical form, in a tragic vision of human beings as insignificant actors on the vast stage of the world:

> Life's but a walking shadow, a poor player
> That struts and frets his hour upon the stage,
> And then is heard no more
>
> (Act 5, Scene 5, lines 24–6)

The theatre for which Shakespeare wrote, however, was very different in design from the theatres of today, and this had many effects on the form and structure of *Macbeth*.

Firstly, the layout of an Elizabethan theatre was unlike most conventional modern theatres, as you will see from the line drawing on page 256. (The period in which Shakespeare wrote tends to be described as 'Elizabethan', even though James I was on the throne between 1603 and Shakespeare's death in 1616.) There were additional acting areas, for example, for which individual lines or whole scenes would be specially written. The conversation between Duncan and Banquo about birds nesting in the castle battlements – which opens Act 1,

Scene 6 – would probably have been directed up towards the balcony. And the inner stage would almost certainly have been used to represent the interior of the witches' den in Act 4.

A structural difference of even greater direct significance to the writing of *Macbeth*, however, was the nearness of the listening audience to the players. The shape of an Elizabethan theatre was octagonal or round (which is why the famous Globe theatre was given its name), which meant that the audience – seated in tiers around the walls – was brought into very close contact with the action. Moreover, the stage itself was not separated from the audience, as it tends to be nowadays. Instead it projected into the pit of the theatre, where the standing audience – or 'groundlings' – was gathered. This increased intimacy made soliloquies or stage whispers a far more natural and believable stage phenomenon than is often true today. A modern Macbeth usually has to bellow the lines:

> Hear it not, Duncan; for it is a knell
> That summons thee to heaven or to hell.
>
> (Act 2, Scene 1, lines 63–4)

at a volume that would awaken all but the soundest of sleepers. Similarly, the secret asides of Malcolm and Donalbain in Act 2, Scene 3 – or of Lady Macbeth during the banquet in Act 3, Scene 4 – can sometimes become crashingly and embarrassingly audible in a modern production.

Another significant feature of the main stage in an Elizabethan theatre was that it had no curtain to indicate changes of act or scene. On a mundane level, this accounts for Shakespeare's tendency to use rhymed couplets to close a scene. A pair of rhymed lines such as:

> Away, and mock the time with fairest show:
> False face must hide what the false heart doth know.
>
> (Act 1, Scene 7, lines 81–2)

indicated to the audience that a particular episode had concluded (some critics suggest that rhymed couplets *within* scenes were also used as a kind of cue system – to wake up any actor who may have dozed off to sleep backstage!). The main thing that we need to be aware of, though, is what we *lose* from *Macbeth* by the use of a stage curtain where none was intended. Act 5, for example, consists of nine short scenes in which – one by one – all the forces of retribution can be seen to be assembling and closing in on Macbeth. He is virtually static, helpless to resist this relentless advance:

> They have tied me to a stake: I cannot fly,
> But, bear-like, I must fight the course . . .
>
> (Act 5, Scene 7, lines 1–2)

Clearly, it is vital to this effect of claustrophobia and inner pressure that all of these scenes should be presented as a sequence of continuous action.

Speed is not the only dramatic effect that can be reduced quite badly by the introduction of curtains or lengthy scene changes. For Shakespeare also wove into the fabric of *Macbeth* an intricate pattern of parallels and contrasts, of echoes and signals, which are seriously weakened by disruption. In Act 3, Scene 2, line 17, for example, Macbeth swears that he is prepared to violate the very order of the universe: 'Ere we will eat our meal in fear . . .'. Yet the events of the subsequent banquet scene, only minutes of stage time later, show the folly and irony of this resolution: the meal is left unfinished. A more sustained example – showing the effect and importance of contrast between whole acts – can be found in the transition between Acts 4 and 5. Again, this really needs to be instant, if its full symbolic potential is to be realized. Act 4 closes in the ordered haven of the English court, where a saintly king has the gift of healing. Act 5, on the other hand, opens in the 'infected' and disordered world of Macbeth's kingdom. The regal blank verse of the previous act has disintegrated into the pathetic prose fragments of Lady Macbeth's madness. And her sickness is so great that the Doctor can do nothing: 'This disease is beyond my practice' (Act 5, Scene 1, line 54).

The sleep-walking scene which opens Act 5 occurs at night. In a modern production this will usually be apparent immediately. Lady Macbeth will be shown performing her strange, sad rituals in the subdued and shadowy lighting of a darkened stage. Elizabethan performances, however, usually took place in the daylight – a fact that often comes as something of a surprise to contemporary readers. Even the most sophisticated, roofed theatres of the Elizabethan age employed none of the resources of lighting and scenery that we have now come to expect. The audience would still understand, of course, that the sleep-walking episode was taking place at night. But their understanding was far more likely to come from the Doctor's opening remark: 'I have two nights watched with you . . .' (Act 5, Scene 1, line 1), and from the candle that Lady Macbeth carries in her hand, than from any real attempt to represent darkness *visually* on stage.

Again, this fundamental difference between Shakespeare's theatre and our own had a considerable influence on the writing of *Macbeth*. When precise details of time are important, for example, they are specified within the script. The witches tell us that they will meet with Macbeth ''ere the set of sun'. Macbeth tells us that the banquet will be held at 'seven at night'. And before the murder of Duncan, a conversation between Banquo and Fleance establishes for the audience that it is after midnight:

BANQUO

How goes the night, boy?

FLEANCE

The moon is down; I have not heard the clock.

BANQUO

And she goes down at twelve.

FLEANCE   I take 't, 't is later, Sir.
                                                    (Act 2, Scene 1, lines 1–3)

But by far the most powerful effect on *Macbeth* of the absence of lighting or scenery is the wonderful wealth of descriptive detail that is therefore concentrated into the *poetry* of the play. It is this, above all else, that gives *Macbeth* its very special atmosphere. Consider, for example, the power of these haunting evocations of night-fall:

> Now o'er the one half world
> Nature seems dead, and wicked dreams abuse
> The curtained sleep: witchcraft celebrates
> Pale Hecate's offerings; and withered Murder,
> Alarumed by his sentinel, the wolf,
> Whose howl's his watch, thus with his stealthy pace,
> With Tarquin's ravishing strides, towards his design
> Moves like a ghost . . .
>
> (Act 2, Scene 1, lines 49–56)

> . . . light thickens; and the crow
> Makes wing to the rooky wood;
> Good things of day begin to droop and drowse,
> Whiles night's black agents to their preys do rouse.
>
> (Act 3, Scene 2, lines 50–3)

Or look at this magical description of sunset:

> The west yet glimmers with some streaks of day:
> Now spurs the lated traveller apace,
> To gain the timely inn . . .
>
> (Act 3, Scene 3, lines 5–7)

Here every single word and sound is uniquely effective. The delicate word 'glimmers' suggests a wistful lingering. The exactness of 'streaks' evokes vividly the thin ribbons of coloured light that pattern the evening sky like paint on fabric. And then how skilfully we are moved from sky to land, from the abstract to the familiar, by the image of the lone traveller seeking shelter.

Conclusion

Macbeth did not begin as a set of printed words on a flat page. It is not a dreary thesis, intended for joyless and sombre study. It was – and is – a living, changing entity – written for performance in the real world, on a real stage, by real people. To learn more about its origins can be both exciting and rewarding. But ultimately – to quote a phrase from the twentieth-century poet, T.S. Eliot – *Macbeth* exists both 'in and out of time'. It is far too great and rich a work ever to be limited to one time, place or meaning.

In the end, the most important things that you will ever learn about it are the things that you will discover for yourself.

Macbeth in performance

(Above) Ian McKellen and Judy Dench as Macbeth and Lady Macbeth in the RSC production at The Other Place in 1976.
(Page 253, top) Peter O'Toole and Frances Tomelty as Macbeth and Lady Macbeth at the Old Vic in 1980.
(Page 253, bottom) Nicol Williamson and Helen Mirren as Macbeth and Lady Macbeth in the RSC production at Stratford in 1974.

(Top) The Young Vic production in 1975.
(Bottom) The RSC production in 1976.

254

Questions

The photographs on pages 252–53 show three different interpretations of Macbeth and Lady Macbeth.

1 At what precise point in the play do you imagine each photograph was taken?
2 What seem to you the main differences between the three portrayals of Lady Macbeth?
  What characteristics are suggested by appearance and costume?
  What do the facial expressions suggest?
3 How do the three portrayals of Macbeth differ?
4 In his essay (page xii), Braham Murray speaks about the love between husband and wife. In which photograph does this seem to you most apparent?
  Do you agree that it *should* be apparent?
5 Which couple most resembles your own imagined view of Macbeth and Lady Macbeth?

The photographs opposite show two different ways of presenting the witches.

1 At what precise point in the play do you imagine each photograph was taken?
2 What specific differences do you find in the two ways of portraying the witches?
3 Which photograph do you find the more sinister, and why?
4 What do you think is the purpose and effect of the masks in the Young Vic production?
5 What do you think is the purpose and effect of modern dress in the RSC production?

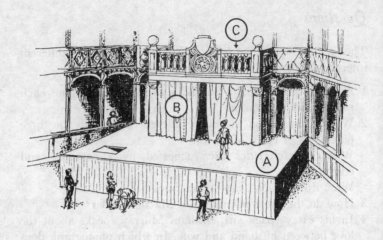

This picture shows a typical stage of Shakespeare's day. The acting areas were:

A the main stage, projecting into the audience;
B the 'inner stage', concealed by curtains when not in use;
C the 'upper stage', or balcony.

With these points in mind, how do you suppose the following scenes might have been staged:

1 the murder of Duncan?
2 the banquet scene?
3 Macbeth's visit to the witches in Act 4?

Macbeth today

The activities which follow are intended to help and encourage modern readers in their study of Macbeth.

Drama

Prophecies Act 1, Scene 3

Bearing in mind Macbeth's reactions during and after his encounter with the witches, devise a play or scene of your own in which someone happens by chance to meet a fortune teller or read a horoscope. Three surprising predictions are made, one of which comes true immediately. . . .

Pretending innocence Act 1, Scene 5

Lady Macbeth tells Macbeth to 'look like the innocent flower/But be the serpent under 't'. Work out a situation that shows someone deliberately behaving very normally while planning to do something wrong, and then pretending to be as shocked as everyone else once it has been done. Now improvise the scene in the following three ways:
1 with no one being at all suspicious;
2 with one of the other characters being very suspicious, but reluctant to accuse the person directly;
3 with one of the other characters being able to *prove* that the person is lying.

Manliness Act 1, Scene 7

Lady Macbeth goads Macbeth into acting against his conscience and better judgement by accusing him of being

257

cowardly and unmanly. Devise a series of three scenes in which
a boy feels compelled to do something he does not really wish
to do in order to appear 'manly' in the eyes of:

1 his girlfriend;
2 his parents;
3 his male friends.

Fear of discovery   Act 3, Scene 1

Macbeth's longing to be '*safely* thus' leads him to order the
murder of his friend. Work out a sequence of scenes which
shows how one crime can lead to another.

A contract to kill   Act 3, Scene 1

Macbeth tries to justify Banquo's murder to the hired
assassins. Improvise a scene in which someone is persuaded
to harm somebody that he or she barely knows. What will be
the main inducement? money? a threat? reasoned argument?

Excuses   Act 3, Scene 4

Lady Macbeth explains Macbeth's erratic behaviour by
inventing an illness he has supposedly had since childhood.
Improvise a scene in which excuses are invented for each of
the following situations:

1 a murderer tries to explain to the police why there are
  bloodstains on his or her jacket;
2 a burglar tries to explain his or her presence in the living
  room at midnight to an angry householder;
3 a pupil tries to explain to the class teacher why he or she
  has done no English homework for two weeks;
4 a teenager tries to explain returning from a party at 8 a.m.
  to a furious parent.

Testing   Act 4, Scene 3

Malcolm tests the character and loyalty of Macduff by pretending to be an unfit ruler. Devise a scene of your own in which one character deliberately tests another by pretending to be irresponsible or untrustworthy.

Guilt   Act 5, Scene 1

Lady Macbeth's sleep-walking reveals her guilt. In what other ways do people give themselves away? Prepare and present a short play in which a character (intentionally or otherwise) finally betrays his or her guilt.

Coursework

Research projects

1 Using library books to help you, compile a time chart of events leading up to, and immediately following, the Gunpowder Plot.
2 Draw the family tree of James I of England, showing how the thrones of Scotland and England came to be united.
3 Make an illustrated booklet about either witches or ghosts.

Creative work

1 Paste up an illustrated front page for the eleventh-century 'Scone Herald', describing the coronation of Macbeth and recounting the tragic events leading up to his succession to the throne.
2 Re-read the opening of Act 4, Scene 1. Suggest alternative contents for a modern-day witches' cauldron, and write your own rhyme to go with them.

259

3 Lady Macbeth does not appear at all in Act 4. Write an imaginary diary for her which covers that period.
4 Write a secret letter from the Doctor to his wife, explaining what is happening at Dunsinane.
5 Choose a short scene or extract from *Macbeth*, and present it as a 20-frame cartoon strip.

Play production dossier

Choose any scene from *Macbeth* and assemble a folder containing the following production notes relating to that scene:
1 a set plan;
2 a list of props, and where they should be placed;
3 costume designs for the actors involved;
4 a lighting plan – including a note of any changes that will occur during the scene;
5 an exact account of the movements, facial expressions and tone of voice throughout the scene of *one* of the major characters. This is probably best done by obtaining a photocopy of the scene and adding your own notes to it in red ink.

Oral work

1 Invent and act out the following extra scenes:
   Act 1: Lady Macbeth plying the chamberlains with drink;
   Act 2: Macbeth committing the murder of Duncan;
   Act 3: the two murderers discussing whether or not to kill Banquo;
   Act 4: the witches commenting on Macbeth's visit and his reactions to the Apparitions;
   Act 5: the Doctor and the Gentlewoman trying to stop Lady Macbeth from killing herself.
2 In pairs, devise and record a four-minute interview in which one of the following characters is questioned by a reporter:
   Act 1: Banquo describes his meeting with the witches;

Act 2: Donalbain describes his reaction to his father's death and explains his decision to run away;

Act 3: Ross describes Macbeth's behaviour at the banquet;

Act 4: Macduff describes his impressions of Malcolm;

Act 5: Malcolm describes how it feels to be King of Scotland and how he intends to rule the country.

3 Imagine that, following the banquet in Act 3, Macbeth and Lady Macbeth are arrested and charged with the murders of Duncan and Banquo. As a class, plan and stage a trial scene. You will need:

a prosecutor;
separate defence lawyers for Macbeth and Lady Macbeth;
witnesses;
a jury;
a judge.

Quizzes

In groups, devise ten additional questions for each of the following quizzes. The first two questions are given as examples.

1 *Who*
   (a) confessed his treason before dying?
   (b) said: 'O, full of scorpions is my mind'?

2 *When*
   (a) did Macbeth discover he was Thane of Cawdor?
   (b) did Lady Macbeth ring a bell?

3 *Why*
   (a) did Lady Macbeth not kill Duncan herself?
   (b) did Macbeth say: 'Accursèd be that tongue that tells me so'?

Games

Work out and make a computer program *or* a card game *or*

a board game based loosely on some of the events in *Macbeth*, with one of the following titles:

1 Murder in the Castle;
2 The Witches' Den;
3 Escape from Birnam Wood.

Essay questions

1 Is Macbeth a hero or a villain in your opinion?
2 Examine the presentation and function of the supernatural in *Macbeth*.
3 Show how Shakespeare's poetry evokes an atmosphere of evil in *Macbeth*.
4 Discuss the importance of references to children and babies in *Macbeth*.
5 To what extent do you think Lady Macbeth should be held responsible for her husband's fate?
6 How do you regard Banquo? Do you consider him to be a wholly admirable and blameless character?
7 Discuss the use Shakespeare makes of soliloquy in *Macbeth*.
8 Explain the importance of the long interview between Macduff and Malcolm in England (Act 4, Scene 3) to *Macbeth* as a whole.
9 What is the significance of eating and sleeping in *Macbeth*?
10 '*Macbeth* teaches us the dangers of trusting that things are always what they seem.' Do you agree?